Praise for I

"What C-Level executives read to keep their edge and make pivotal business decisions. Timeless classics for indispensable knowledge." - Richard Costello, Manager-Corporate Marketing Communication, General Electric (NYSE: GE)

"Want to know what the real leaders are thinking about now? It's in here." - Carl Ledbetter, SVP & CTO, Novell, Inc.

"Priceless wisdom from experts at applying technology in support of business objectives." - Frank Campagnoni, CTO, GE Global Exchange Services

"Unique insights into the way the experts think and the lessons they've learned from experience." - MT Rainey, Co-CEO, Young & Rubicam/Rainey Kelly Campbell Roalfe

"Unlike any other business book." - Bruce Keller, Partner, Debevoise & Plimpton

"The Inside the Minds series is a valuable probe into the thought, perspectives, and techniques of accomplished professionals. By taking a 50,000 foot view, the authors place their endeavors in a context rarely gleaned from text books or treatiese." - Chuck Birenbaum, Partner, Thelen Reid & Priest

"A must read for anyone in the industry." - Dr. Chuck Lucier, Chief Growth Officer, Booz-Allen & Hamilton

"A must read for those who manage at the intersection of business and technology." - Frank Roney, General Manager, IBM

"A great way to see across the changing marketing landscape at a time of significant innovation." - David Kenny, Chairman & CEO, Digitas

"An incredible resource of information to help you develop outside-the-box..." - Rich Jernstedt, CEO, Golin/Harris International

"A snapshot of everything you need..." - Charles Koob, Co-Head of Litigation Department, Simpson Thacher & Bartlet

www.Aspatore.com

Aspatore Books is the largest and most exclusive publisher of C-Level executives (CEO, CFO, CTO, CMO, Partner) from the world's most respected companies. Aspatore annually publishes a select group of C-Level executives from the Global 1,000, top 250 professional services firms, law firms (Partners & Chairs), and other leading companies of all sizes. C-Level Business Intelligence™, as conceptualized and developed by Aspatore Books, provides professionals of all levels with proven business intelligence from industry insiders – direct and unfiltered insight from those who know it best – as opposed to third-party accounts offered by unknown authors and analysts. Aspatore Books is committed to publishing a highly innovative line of business books, and redefining such resources as indispensable tools for all professionals. In addition to individual best-selling business titles, Aspatore Books publishes the following lines of unique books, reports and journals: Inside the Minds, Executive Reports, and C-Level Quarterly Journals. Aspatore is a privately held company headquartered in Boston, Massachusetts, with employees around the world.

Inside the Minds

The critically acclaimed *Inside the Minds* series provides readers of all levels with proven business intelligence from C-Level executives (CEO, CFO, CTO, CMO, Partner) from the world's most respected companies. Each chapter is comparable to a white paper or essay and is a future-oriented look at where an industry/profession/topic is heading and the most important issues for future success. Each author has been carefully chosen through an exhaustive selection process by the *Inside the Minds* editorial board to write a chapter for this book. *Inside the Minds* was conceived in order to give readers actual insights into the leading minds of business executives worldwide. Because so few books or other publications are actually written by executives in industry, *Inside the Minds* presents an unprecedented look at various industries and professions never before available.

INSIDE THE MINDS

Inside the Minds:
The Art of Retail
Industry CEOs on Successfully Delivering Product to Market

Published by Aspatore, Inc.
For corrections, company/title updates, comments or any other inquiries please email info@aspatore.com.

First Printing, 2003
10 9 8 7 6 5 4 3 2 1

ISBN 1-58762-237-8

Library of Congress Control Number: 2003112415

Inside the Minds Managing Editor, Carolyn Murphy, Edited by Michaela Falls, Proofread by Eddie Fournier, Cover design by Scott Rattray & Ian Mazie

Inside the Minds:
The Art of Retail
Industry CEOs on Successfully Delivering Product to Market

CONTENTS

A New Brand of Retail

James W. Keyes
7-Eleven, Inc.
President & CEO

Convenience Retail

At 7-Eleven, we have a very unique perspective on the business of convenience retailing. After literally inventing the industry, through the past 76 years we have had to evolve to survive. The art of keeping pace with changing needs of the convenience customer – at least at 7-Eleven – is not so much art as it is science.

That's not to say that retail – or science – is cold or clinical. In its purest form, science is not just the assemblage of data. It is the interpretation of that data, the ability to modify actions and then the measurement of those results that makes retailing a science. Actually, good retailing is successfully bringing the products to market that customers want through the science of data interpretation (that allows for identification and development of new products) and the art of communication (that allows for the customer to know the difference).

In the Beginning

7-Eleven started 76 years ago in Dallas, Texas, with an ice dock. The company sold big blocks of ice. At the time, we did not have technology, but we had the eyes and ears of that retailer who knew each of his customers by name. When a customer told the retailer that they had just bought a refrigerator and would not be back for blocks of ice, the retailer was smart enough to modify his product assortment. He realized that if he did not address the product assortment issue, he would not sell any more blocks of ice because people were buying refrigerators. So the retailer began to sell ice and milk. Before long, he increased his product assortment to ice, milk, and bread.

That ability for a retailer to use consumer behavior information to change product assortment not only gave birth to an industry (the convenience industry as we know it today), but also represented retailing in its purest form. Retailing is understanding the changing needs of the customer, and modifying your behavior to keep up with those changing needs. Today, with technology, we have the ability to monitor the sales of every item, everyday, at every store. By harnessing that data, we have gone back to the purest form of retailing. We call it "retailer initiative."

Changes in the Convenience World

Technology can be an enabler for all retailers. It makes possible everything from faster point-of-sale transactions, to providing item-by-item data for better management of product assortment, to providing cost efficiencies. Because of the ability to do all of those things, technology enables us to be better retailers.

It would be easy to look at behemoth retailers like Wal-Mart and 7-Eleven and suggest that the personal element of retailing is falling by the wayside. Instead, technology can help us keep that personal element in place. The difference is in how we obtain and use the information. In 1927, it was a store owner talking to a customer he knew by name. Today, in twenty-five thousand 7-Eleven stores around the globe, more customers walk through the doors in one hour than that first store operator saw in an entire year. The only way to capture that amount of data on customers' needs is through the efficient use of technology.

Within 7-Eleven, we are now able to harness the information and to put it in the hands of individual store operators. The store operator can be more of an entrepreneur than ever before, now armed with more effective decision making tools. I believe this is bringing retail full circle. At 7-Eleven, retail initiative involves leveraging the scale and the power of our unique distribution system and putting it in the hands of entrepreneurs at the store level, who can tailor their individual stores' product assortment to the needs of the neighborhood. We bring all of the buying power and the global brand capability of a Wal-Mart, and we put it in the hands of an individual neighborhood operator – one who is very focused on customer service.

In convenience retail, customer service is first and foremost defined by having those products in stock that customers want and need – otherwise, we would not be convenient. If the customer comes into a store with a brand preference, product preference, or emergency need, and we are not there for them, we become inconvenient. Our definition of customer service starts with product assortment and having the right products available 24 hours a day.

Then, of course, the service side of the business is also very important. We call it fast, friendly service – the ability to get customers in and out very quickly, hopefully with a smile.

Like many retailers, we measure our customer service performance in terms of what we call the five fundamentals of convenience retail. At 7-Eleven, those fundamentals are (1) product assortment, (2) quality, (3) cleanliness, (4) fast and friendly service, and (5) value. We literally measure each of our stores on the basis of those five fundamentals of convenience. All the technology and data in the world is useless unless it's applied on behalf of customer satisfaction.

Goals for the Company

We have an opportunity to become the best retailer in the world. It is indeed, an ambitious goal. The unique opportunity of 7–Eleven is not only our global scale, but also our upside potential if we successfully hone the retail skill of thousands of new entrepreneurs (i.e., individual store operators) each year. 7-Eleven has a bit of a unique structure in that we have the opportunity to create individual entrepreneurs who are franchisees. If the business model is successful, the potential to attract new franchisees is virtually unlimited. Our challenge now is to perfect this business model at each individual store. It must work successfully for both the franchisee and the corporation at the individual store level. That involves a process of reinventing the store and the company, which is what we have been doing for the last ten years.

We also have sales goals and profit goals for each store. Basically, I hope to get to a point where each store's performance can emulate the performance of the whole corporation. Our corporation today is not as vertically integrated as it once was. My commitment to shareholders is to increase return on invested capital with total revenue growth. The same goal should apply to each individual store, having each improve its return on invested capital for that location, and improve in-store sales growth at that location. If each store is achieving those goals, the success of the entire enterprise is assured.

Impact of Economic Changes on Retailing

Retailers have always made the same excuses through eternity. Back in the markets of ancient Greece, on a rainy day, they probably blamed poor sales on the rain. But if you're good at retailing, you will figure out how to sell something that people need on a rainy day, a sunny day, a good day or bad. One of my favorite examples is evident in the streets of New York City; when it starts to rain, it takes about five minutes before hundreds of vendors are on every street corner selling umbrellas. That's retailing at its finest: keeping up with the changing needs of the customer. If the retailer can be that quick to respond to customer changes, who cares if it rains?

The same thing goes for a tough economy; people still have needs in a tough economy. The question is how their needs will change and whether we are fast enough or nimble enough to respond to those needs. 7-Eleven has enjoyed between 4 and 5 percent same-store sales increases for much of the last 5 years, in the good economy and then in a troubled economy. We have achieved that stability in merchandise sales by keeping up with changes in customer needs. When the economy changed in the third quarter of the year 2000, we saw a sharp change in our consumer buying powers. We discovered that our traffic count was the same, but customers were buying less, or they were buying different products. The twelve-pack beer customer was shifting to a six-pack or single beer. The gallon milk person was shifting to a half-gallon.

If you look at the dramatically rising gasoline prices at the time, the disposable spending of the average customer decreased by as much as $50 a month. If your driving doesn't change, and the price of gasoline increases $0.40 per gallon, you have as much as $50 less spending money this month than you had last month. The average person who makes $30,000 to $35,000 a year, has an apartment, and has a family to feed, doesn't have much more than a few hundred dollars left each month. So, if you lose $50, you're forced to change what you do.

Because of the data that we track every single day, we saw consumer buying patterns change. We then modified our product assortment to meet the customers' new needs. Instead of merchandising gallon milk, we changed our whole assortment to feature half-gallons. Instead of selling twelve-pack beer as we had done for twenty years, we changed our product assortment to offer a whole door of single beers. When we changed our product mix, the customers responded by buying in different ways. Same store sales, of course, responded favorably.

Finding and Training the Right People

I compare the "people" challenge to the "product assortment" challenge. Finding and retaining good people is much like good merchandising. We have to create demand on the product side. If I just put products on the shelf, and I don't have the right products or the right quality, the only way I can sell those products is to drop the price. I can stimulate demand artificially, but I cannot sustain that demand. If you translate that into people, it works similarly. I can attract people by paying a higher salary. It's like using price to drive product. The competition can come in and match a salary, and steal those people away. Instead, I have to create demand that is based on more than lower price or higher salary. On the product side, I have to create demand for the right products and the right quality. On the people side of the equation, I have to have the right job. I have to have a work environment that is compelling, interesting, and intellectually stimulating for an employee.

Retail is one of the most fascinating career opportunities. We all like feedback and with retail, you can get immediate feedback. If people are just ringing up sales, they don't get much feedback. But, if they are managing a section of the store, they are really being retailers; they are ordering and making product assortment decisions. They are trying to figure out how the customer is going to react to a change in the way a product is merchandised, or the presence of a new product entirely. Every day, they face the merchandise challenge in the store. Again with technology as an enabler, we can actually make that job – inside a 7-Eleven store – educational and satisfying. It's fun to go to work because you are challenged every day with a new set of uncertainties about how the customer will react, and you are given the power to make decisions at the store level so that tomorrow you can see the results of your decisions. So, it is much more interesting than just standing at a cash register ringing up sales.

We are also in the early stages of developing advanced training accessible at store level. Due to our size and turnover, it is a constant challenge to keep employees abreast of the changes and improvements we bring to our system. We now have streaming video capabilities that can be transmitted to each store, so someone can be trained right at the sales counter behind the cash register. They can watch the training module that teaches them how to ring up a sale, how to run a cash register, how to manage a section of the store. Those are further examples of the use of technology that will continue to make it easier for us to attract, train and retain the best possible employees.

Leadership vs. Management

Over the years, I have come to understand the difference between management and leadership. In the role of a CEO, I try to demonstrate more leadership, because my job is increasingly one of governance, which is a much different challenge than day-to-day management. The challenge comes in knowing when to manage and when to lead. If I have good people who are aligned strategically and who are meeting their performance objectives, then I can be more of a leader, and less hands-on. If, however, I have people who are not carrying their end of the bargain or are failing to meet their objectives and are not strategically aligned, then I have to get much more involved. I then roll up my sleeves and dive into whatever level of detail is necessary to make sure that we move the whole enterprise forward. Therefore, I have frequent applications of both management styles.

I try to make executives and managers feel empowered. At 7-Eleven, we have an approach that we think of as "centralized decentralization." In other words, as a global company, we want to leverage our scale, so many decisions must be made centrally. There are certain advantages that you can gain in buying and sourcing products that way. If we were to simply turn everyone loose and let them do their own thing, we would never be able to leverage our scale. When it comes to product assortment decisions, however, we encourage individual store managers or franchisees to act as entrepreneurs, to be empowered. It's important that they not only feel empowered, but that they actually are empowered. They have the opportunity to make decisions within a reasonable spectrum that we have provided. It is not unlimited "free-range" entrepreneurialism, but "managed" entrepreneurialism. At the store level, there is a lot of ability to tailor individual stores. Any store can choose from some 5,000 to 6,000 products, the 2,000 that best meet the needs of their neighborhood. Then they can go out and find another group of products that are very unique to their neighborhood. It might be an ethnic product – for instance, a rice product in an Asian market that they can source locally.

Changes in Retail

From time to time, especially during troubled economic times, some adverse changes happen in retail. I've seen many retailers commoditize products relying on discounting and price promotions to bolster sales. I believe that that's what good merchants can do. Many retailers who have used price as a tool for retailing have caused other retailers to believe that it is the only tool. I look at Wal-Mart, and I wonder if it's the price or the greeting at the door or the assortment that they have, that makes them so successful. Well, it's a combination of all those things. If you look at it superficially, you could leap to the conclusion that it is price alone. In reality, it is far more than price that makes up the Wal-Mart shopping experience. If other retailers try to compete on the basis of price but don't have a consistent low cost cap ability, they can find themselves in fairly serious trouble. Unfortunately, retailers tend to follow other retailers. So many jump on the price bandwagon; products that could have significant value associated with them can become commodities very quickly.

One of the most interesting phenomena that I have seen is the aggressive price promotion of twelve-pack soft drinks. Twelve-pack soft drinks have been used for many years as a loss leader to draw customers. You can often buy Coca-Cola or Pepsi at a price much less than that of bottled water. But think of the inconsistency there. These are two of the best brands in the world that should capture a premium price. Are these products really effective as loss leaders or is it a lost opportunity? I hope all retailers will ponder ways to add value consistently. It is always easy to create a commodity out of a product, but to add value is a much more challenging proposition. That's what good retailers are all about.

I predict some huge changes in supply-chain efficiencies. At 7-Eleven, we affectionately refer to the supply chain as a "demand" chain. We start with what the customer wants and work backward to the manufacturer, with the objective being to try to eliminate some of the inefficiencies. Retail distribution is extremely inefficient – a byproduct of an industry that started with small mom-and-pop stores. The suppliers or manufacturers have a challenge to distribute to a widely fragmented and widely dispersed group of locations. Today, however, companies that are much more national or international in scale have the ability to gain much greater supply-chain efficiencies that will help both the manufacturers and retailers. Ultimately, we're going to be putting better, fresher products in the consumers' hands.

I believe the industry is changing, and as we change, I am encouraged by seeing more competition. In other countries, our competition at retail is terrific. There are some very strong competitors, and it creates a better overall marketplace than we see here in the United States. We have very little organized competition here for convenience retail. Most of the industry is fragmented. I hope to see the trend toward some consolidation among other retailers. Overall, I believe that a healthier competitive environment with stronger national players will be better for retail.

Changing the Consumer Mindset

One of the present challenges that we face is the changing mindset of the American consumer as it relates to the importance of freshness. We have built an infrastructure to be able to produce fresh baked goods – fresh doughnuts, fresh muffins, fresh croissants – every single day for our stores, and yet, we see customers walking into our stores and choosing instead packaged product. They have the perception that longer shelf life is better, so they buy the packaged product as an alternative.

Here we are breaking into a new, emerging business based on healthier alternatives to fast food, for example, a turkey and cheese sandwich with lettuce and tomato that is made today has a 24 hour shelf life. Yet, a consumer will pick it up, read that it expires today, and put it back on the shelf thinking that the prepackaged sandwich next to it, with a seven-day shelf life, is better. There is a huge perception change that we have to create, beginning with our own obsession with quality. Fresh is always better; if we eventually prove to our consumers that the food in the case is fresher than the seven-day packaged sandwich, then they will respond.

Taking Risks to Grow

Risk in product management and advertising really comes down to responsible decision-making. If we do enough research and testing, then we minimize the amount of risk that we are asking our shareholders to withstand. Business is about making investments in order to grow, and as we make those investments, we must make those investments with sound judgment. But, we do have to take risks; if we don't take any risks, it is difficult to grow. One of the advantages of 7-Eleven is that we see our stores as 25,000 laboratories. At any given time, if something works in one store, we can pick it up and drop it into another store anywhere else in the world and see if it's going to be a worldwide success, a nationwide success, or a market-by-market success.

Many retailers over the years have abdicated retailing to suppliers. They've given up their valuable shelf space by turning retail outlets into real estate. They sell shelf space in the form of slotting allowances and retail allowances to manufacturers. Then, they have little space in which to manage and, therefore, to satisfy consumers' needs. They're giving up their privilege or right as retailers to someone upstream (a supplier or manufacturer). But the question is whether we are in the retail business or the real estate business. Good retailers presumably can make more informed decision about their shelf space than anyone else. I'm trying to put that decision as close to the consumers as I possibly can: into the hands of that individual store operator.

Big Box vs. Little Box

Not every trend in retailing suggests that bigger is better. While the hyper-markets and discounters drive business via bulk-buying, the customer still craves convenience. Convenience stores can be more nimble and cater to the needs of customers in their immediate trade area without compromising quality or value.

Convenience store staff can create a personal relationship with their customers in an increasingly impersonal world. Traditional department and grocery stores may eventually find themselves in a compromising position – unable to compete on price with the Wal-Marts of the world or the convenience and service of a neighborhood 7-Eleven.

Constant Change Key to Success

In any retail environment, success comes down to understanding your customers' needs. As simple as that may sound, it is actually a very challenging proposition. Definitions of value will differ; for some it will be heavily weighted toward price, and for others – as in our case – toward convenience and availability of products. For others, it might be brand and freshness. We all have to find a definition of value that works and creates economic return for us as retailers, by satisfying the customers' demands.

Probably the most important aspect of retail is the ability to change constantly. There is only one thing that is consistent about consumer demand, and that is, that it is consistently changing; it will change over and over again. We've discovered that convenience reaches across many more age groups and demographic groups than the old definition – beer, soft drinks, and beef jerky – did. We can supply needs from prepaid phone cards to Internet banking to fresh foods. We now offer a wide range of goods and services that we never thought we could provide before.

In its most simplistic terms, success is about generating shareholder value. The retail industry has never been the darling of the investment community, for a whole host of reasons. I believe that the investment community – if they see a different approach to retail that allows us to create growth and improve return on investment capital – could become much greater supporters of retail and could help the industry to thrive. But is has to start with us as retailers, and we have a job to do. We have an industry to transform, hopefully together. Over time, we want to create a healthier environment for all of us. I enjoy retail because of the challenge of meeting the changing needs of the customer, which makes this a tremendously dynamic industry, and one that I find compelling.

Jim Keyes is president and chief executive officer for 7-Eleven, Inc., the world's largest convenience store retailer. Mr. Keyes served in a number of senior management positions before being elected to his current role in 2000. He joined 7-Eleven stores' former subsidiary Citgo Petroleum in 1985 as general manager of marketing and business strategy. A year later, he became general manager of 7-Eleven's national gasoline, with responsibility for the company's retail gasoline business in the United States and Canada. He was named vice president of national gasoline in 1991. Before joining 7-Eleven, he held various field and corporate positions at Gulf Oil Corporation.

Mr. Keyes served as the company's senior financial officer in 1992 and was named chief financial officer in 1995. He was elected to the company's board of directors in 1997 and promoted to executive vice president and chief operating officer in 1998.

Mr. Keyes is founding chairman of Education is Freedom, a public charity dedicated to helping hard-working young people reach their full potential through higher education. He serves on the national board of directors of Students in Free Enterprise (SIFE), the Muscular Dystrophy Association, Latino Initiatives for the Next Century (LINC) and on the board of trustees for the Boys and Girls Club. Mr. Keyes also is on the board of directors for the National Association of Convenience Stores (NACS). He was recognized by the Network of Executive Women for his efforts to promote diversity in the workplace. Mr. Keyes serves in a leadership role within the local Dallas community as well, as an executive board member of the Greater Dallas Chamber of Commerce, a member of the Dallas Citizens Council and a member of Southern Methodist University's Cox School of Business and chairman of the Dallas Symphony Association.

Mr. Keyes earned a Bachelor of Arts degree at Holy Cross College in Worcester, Mass., where he was named to the Phi Beta Kappa honor society and graduated cum laude in 1977. He also attended the University of London and received a Master's of Business Administration degree from Columbia University in New York City.

7-Eleven, Inc. is the premier name and largest chain in the convenience retailing industry. Headquartered in Dallas, Texas, 7-Eleven, Inc. operates or franchises approximately 5,800 7-Eleven® stores in the United States and Canada and licenses approximately 19,500 7-Eleven stores in 17 countries throughout the world. During 2002, 7-Eleven stores worldwide generated total sales of more than $33 billion. Find out more online at www.7-Eleven.com.

The Successful Online Retailer

R. Whitney Anderson

MotherNature.com
Chairman & CEO

Online Retailing: A (Very) Brief History

In the late 1990s, there was so much hype surrounding online retailing that what makes it a fundamentally compelling business was often obscured beneath a veneer of new media buzz. New terms leapt into the public consciousness and became part of accepted business vernacular. Unprecedented levels of capital were poured into Internet start-ups. The major stock indexes skyrocketed. It seemed like a new world had come to pass in which many of the old rules did not apply.

Unfortunately, most people learned the hard way that the old rules had become old for a reason.

When all of the hype was stripped away and the venture capital market dried up, many online retailers were forced to close their doors. What did we learn from this frenzied $50+ billion commercial experiment? We learned that the difference between success and failure is not determined by the creation of new rules, but is determined by adherence to the old rules, and to new ways in which to apply them. In online retailing, poor management, undisciplined spending, and unrealistic expectations are as sure a recipe for disaster as they are offline.

At heart, online retailing is not different from traditional offline retailing. In the end, you are in business to turn a profit. To do that, you need a solid consumer base. You need to sell something customers want. You need to be aware of what your competitors are doing. And you need to give customers excellent service at a competitive price. Online retailers may emphasize certain aspects of their business differently than they would if they were offline, but in essence it is safe to say that the basics of retailing are the same as they ever were and ever shall be.

With that said, it is important to emphasize that there *are* significant differences in the way that some of the old rules are applied. What is different – and this is what makes online retailing exciting – is the speed at which changes occur, and can be made to occur; and the depth of information available to retailers. In our haste to redress the mistakes of the 90s, it is important that we do not throw out the proverbial baby with the bath water. Indeed, many of the tools and techniques that first gained widespread acceptance amidst the hype of the 90s online retail boom, have themselves become valid business techniques that will continue to stand the test of time.

Data mining and analysis, dynamic response and test marketing, interactive customer service, and viral and cooperative promotional techniques have all become standard practices for successful online retailers; the smartest of whom use those techniques along with traditional offline retail business models to ultimately develop long-term, high-growth businesses.

The ability to use those techniques to define a successful online retail strategy often comes down to the speed with which retailers can respond to the abundance of information available to them and their ability to find new and innovative ways to utilize that information. Not only knowing your individual customer's needs, but also being able to anticipate those needs is key. Of course, no two businesses are exactly alike and each retailer has to find their own path to success. Some businesses focus on an exclusive product line, others attempt niche segmentation, and still others, like MotherNature.com, offer a value-added service with their retail operations.

MotherNature.com: Playing to our Strengths
A Survivor's Story

MotherNature.com is an Internet-only retailer. About half of our products are health and alternative health related, from vitamins and herbs to homeopathic remedies. The other half of our product line consists of natural personal care items, including bath and beauty, and exercise and fitness products (such as yoga). It is a wide range of products, to be sure, but they are linked in that they all naturally benefit the health of our customers. In addition to our product line, MotherNature.com also offers an extensive health library to the general public. Within this library, anyone can do research into thousands of health concerns and find out the best ways to prevent and treat those issues.

MotherNature.com has been through a lot in its eight years of existence. Starting off as an offline natural foods store called Mother Nature's General Store, the company went online in 1995. The site went through several rounds of venture capital and an IPO in 1999, raising a total of $140 million. In that time, there were several years of excellent growth, but they were coupled with massive losses as spending far outstripped revenue. With 210 people, significant fixed overhead expenses, intense competition in the sector, and narrowing margins, the management team realized in December 2000 that it would not be able to generate a reasonable return on investment and would better serve shareholders by conducting an orderly liquidation of the company's assets. Believing the brand was a powerful one, we (the Naturalist Network) acquired the assets and relaunched the site and business shortly thereafter. By applying an entirely different business model, outsourcing the non-core functions, creating a much leaner infrastructure, reducing the product SKU count from 30,000 to only the 8,500 most popular, and by utilizing many of the "old" rules of retail, we were able to bring the company to cash-flow positive within 3 months.

Our Management Strategy

Part of what we learned from the mistakes of the past is that in online retailing, a company needs to be flexible, responsive and quick to adapt. For us, in terms of hierarchy, a fairly flat management style has worked best. It's a challenge to have technologists, marketing executives, and operations people sit down and come up with a project game plan when there may be a 40-year age difference between them and when each has a different perspective and skill set but each is so entirely dependent upon the others. A decentralized, group-driven decision-making environment makes for a much more motivated and active management team and helps us to meet our challenge to be quick, flexible and more responsive.

This is key because of the incredible speed at which the industry moves. Offline, it can easily take two years to create and define a store concept, analyze the local markets, identify and choose a location, negotiate the leases, complete the store build-out, merchandise it, and promote the Grand Opening event. Online, that entire life cycle has been reduced to six months. To deal with the pace of our business, cooperative group decision-making is essential.

Another key management tenet for all of our people is to stay on top of the knowledge curve. Information is the key to our business and we have a tremendous amount of information available to us. On the most basic level, we have to know what is selling and why; what's not selling and why; how the marketplace is shifting; how news and research affect our business; and what new products will meet the demands of our customers. There are literally hundreds of variables that can change on a daily basis. And because we can, in large measure, find out what those changes are, and, even better, anticipate them, we devote tremendous energy and resources to staying ahead of the curve.

We use everything at our disposal, from a poll with a few questions, to focus groups and direct customer feedback. Since it's such a vast consumer base – over a million consumers – we get feedback constantly. We try to improve customers' experience on the site based on what they tell us, both good and bad. We try to listen for any frustration that arises. Whether a retailer has to organize 1,000 or 35,000 products, it can be difficult for a consumer to find exactly what he or she is looking for. There's no perfect way to do that, but we've tried to enlist customer advisory teams and individuals who have experience in the area from the offline industry to give us as much feedback as possible. We use a combination of customers and experts in the field to help us refine our web presence and our response to shifting marketplace variables.

In combining a flexible, quick-to-adapt decision-making hierarchy with an intensive focus on information analysis and rapid response capability, we have created an organization that constantly seeks to maximize opportunities while learning from what we've done in the past. This management strategy has helped us to achieve a sense of stability and is the primary driver of our top and bottom-line growth, which averages over 20 percent per month. But we've still got a lot more work to do.

Going Forward: Our Goals

As is the case with many online retail survivors, our primary goal is simply to grow our top line and our free cash flow. Secondarily, and this would be the means through which to achieve our primary goal, we want to continue the 20 percent month over month growth rate. These are the most tangible measures of our business's worth. One cannot have a truly sustainable business without truly sustainable revenues and cash flow. As an objective measure of a plan, if you can be cash-flow positive, even in difficult times and environments, it means that something is empirically solid and sustainable about your business. Ultimately, our cash flow is the most important thing to us. It helps us improve what we have. If we know customers are coming to us and purchasing, and that each purchase on average is contributing to our cash flow, it is also a vote of confidence.

It is always important for us to utilize specific metrics to measure our customers' experience and satisfaction on our site, and use those metrics to stay focused on and improve our core competencies. We use metrics to measure many aspects of our business, some as simple as tracking repeat versus first-time purchaser trends, and others a little more specific, such as tracking the frequency of certain searched keywords to help us anticipate inventory shortfalls. We follow many financial and operational metrics carefully, as well as metrics on an individual customer level that indicate whether we're being successful in our promotions, merchandising, marketing, and customer service. Analyzing all of these measurements provide an objective way of determining whether what we're doing is working for a customer or not. It is our goal to continue to hone our performance and improve those areas where customers may experience any frustration or where they feel we fall short of their expectations.

Looking at a more intangible aspect, our specific goal is to be the single most preferred and trusted natural health resource on the Internet for consumers. The information we have is our biggest draw. Although the information is a cost to us, we have worked for five or six years with leading naturopaths and other credible third-party sources of information to develop a resource that puts us in a leadership position in the industry. The most wonderful aspect of this resource is that if someone has a question, it's not MotherNature.com saying what he or she should do; instead we're providing the best information available in the industry – information that is authoritative, independent, and trustworthy. Based on this idea, a lot of people do come to us to do research. From that research, there's a natural progression to buy products. The draw in our business model is the information and, secondarily, providing a breadth of products. For some of our competitors, the draw would be discounted pricing, or for others it would be just having a branded name. Each model has worked well for some, though we believe that some approaches are less sustainable than others.

The Ten Elements of a Successful Online Retailer

The Internet is littered with the remains of hundreds, if not thousands, of retailers who failed to build successful and sustainable businesses. The reasons for this are manifold; youth, hubris, poor planning, and almost inconceivably, too much money, seem to have been behind many of the failures of the last ten years. Again, there seemed to be a sense among many that the old rules didn't apply. Online retailers like Pets.com and Kosmo.com, blew through millions of dollars in months, without having a realistic plan to turn a profit. Some were lost trying to pursue the Amazon model – selling a diverse and ever-expanding product line and spending millions to build the brand with the hope that in the longer run the profits would materialize. With the notable exception of Amazon, very few, if any, were successful pursuing this model. Others, like Buy.com, stated in their prospectus "We sell a substantial portion of our products at very low prices. As a result, we have extremely low and sometimes negative gross margins on our product sales." This is the classic "sell the dollar for eighty cents" model that many legitimate online retailers were founded on. Unfortunately, you can't make up for these margins in volume. And still others, like Boo.com, a clothing retailer that burned through $130 million, seemed to be carried away by simply too much cash given to young and inexperienced managers. The net result of all this was literally billions of dollars spent on online retailers that failed. The lesson learned is one of caution. The essential dynamics of business never change. Whether you are an online business manager at a Fortune 500 company or an entrepreneur armed with only a business plan, a realistic and detailed strategy combined with strict adherence to disciplined spending is the best blueprint for success.

1) Start with Financial Discipline
Businesspeople, entrepreneurs in particular, generally fall somewhere between optimistic and delusional. It's an important characteristic that will prevent many from throwing in the towel when the odds seem overwhelmingly against them. But this sometime strength, unfortunately, can also be a weakness when it clouds business people's judgment and financial discipline – particularly when the numbers aren't as lofty as their expectations and vision.

The best advice I've received in any industry and in any endeavor is to start with financial discipline. Set out a very strict budget with a clear understanding of what initial investment is needed to test the model and the market. Be extremely strict about making that work and be austere in using your budgeted funds. It's very easy for a businessperson to buy into a vision and end up structuring a business that isn't properly capitalized, overspending in hopes of a market turn, or spending their marketing budget on unfounded and untested marketing campaigns. The businessperson has to go back to the market for more capital only to end up a minor shareholder, or the process becomes a simple exercise in futility and frustration. Create a detailed budget before a penny is spent and stick to the budget in a very disciplined way. Keep ROI projections realistic and always include a cushion to get you through unanticipated market swings or to deal with problems your predecessors or competitors may have experienced. That advice has worked very well for MotherNature.com and has kept us out of the black holes in which some of the "e-tailers" mentioned above have found themselves.

2) Test the Concept Exhaustively
The beauty of the Internet, in my mind, is that it's the ultimate test market medium. A retailer can test an individual product, a marketing

approach, or an individual promotion extensively before taking it out to their full customer base. This is true right down to the writing of a subject line of your newsletter. It can also help definitively determine the difference in response to your new product from a mother of 2 living in suburban Dallas versus a single woman living downtown. In this business, it's so easy to test various strategies until you get it right, that it is surprising that businesses in this industry continue to fail in droves. There's no need to spend huge sums of money until you find the right mix of product and put your overall plan to the test. It's something that really hasn't been done offline, because it is extremely expensive to do. Online, it's not easy to do, but it's something that should be done because the results are worth it. Test marketing is one of the most effective and cost efficient tools in the online retailer's arsenal. In practice, test marketing can save online retailers millions and help build a business from the ground-up based on proven successes.

3) Create a Predictable and Flexible Supply Chain

Inventory management and warehousing are two of the biggest problems plaguing online retailers. To handle this aspect of your business well there are several things to think about. You must choose the right product mix and negotiate good prices for those items. This is, obviously, essential to any business, but has particular importance for online retailers. Another key is to be sure that you have optimal levels of inventory on hand. Knowing what your customers want, and ensuring a speedy and uninterrupted supply of those products can mean the difference between success and failure. You must ensure that your suppliers can manufacture and deliver your product line in a predictable and timely fashion, and that virtually all of your orders are correctly picked and shipped to your customers. The dangers of handling this aspect of your business poorly can lead to out-of-stock items, mis-packed shipments, partial order delivery and ultimately, highly disgruntled customers. Anything that can be done to avoid forcing a customer (or retailer) to pay multiple shipping charges should be. Fulfillment, shipping, and restocking fees alone have broken many an online retailer.

If you already have a store and are going to be picking products out of existing inventory, you have a good start, but are up against a very unique set of concerns. Make sure your suppliers are ready to deal with quick delivery of a single product to help you deal with the inevitable run on certain items. If you're set up with an in-store promotion that has previously worked exceptionally well in the online world, one of your pleased customers will inevitably post that promotion on a popular chat board and you'll sell out of your entire inventory in a day.

If you are brave enough to embark on setting up your own warehouse, purchasing your own inventory, hiring people to pick and pack the orders, your first issue is sufficient capitalization. Don't start out too thinly capitalized or expect to raise money along the way. The capital markets are not kind to e-tailers and raising equity is, at best, unpredictable.

4) Choose Your Technical Platform Wisely
Many third party platforms and services exist to run your online store, whether you're a start-up or a Fortune 500 company. The technical platform of an online retailer is what an interior build-out, plumbing, electricity and POS system is to an offline store. The expense of changing it after it is built is extremely costly and any person or company starting an online retailer will wish to research this well. By failing to do due diligence on the technical platform your company will be built on, you may wind up without a business at all.

5) Build in Scalability
If you've studied the market carefully and are certain there is a demand for your product, you will open your store and, in the first month, can just as easily sell one product or 1,000 products. Offline stores simply

don't have the same problem because sales are invariably dependent on the foot traffic around that particular location. Offline retailers can easily conduct traffic analyses by simply having someone sit at that corner location and count the number of pedestrians and cars that pass by in a given day or week. Online, there are few ways to predict next month's, much less next year's, foot traffic. Fortunately, if you have set up your systems with scalability in mind, it is quite a bit easier to add servers to accommodate more visitors than it is to construct an expansion to your store. Caution is the watchword here. Start small and build progressively and you will set yourself up for long-term success.

6) Take Privacy & Security Seriously

Often the first casualty to being undercapitalized is improper privacy and security protection. According to a poll conducted by Harris Interactive, 90 percent of online customers are concerned about the privacy of their personal data. And 69 percent agree that they have lost control over how their personal information is collected and used by online companies. These numbers are startling. The privacy and confidentiality of someone's purchases is critical in building strong relationships with customers. For online retailers, this is particularly important. Not only in protecting what customers buy, but also in protecting the security with which customers actually complete a transaction. The smarter hackers become, the more difficult it is, and the more important it becomes to make sure all that information is one hundred percent secure.

Ensuring security online is largely a technical issue. Building a team of technical people with the know-how to troubleshoot, test, and retest security systems is essential. At the very least, make sure your reporting mechanism alerts you to the first instances of unauthorized attempts to get into our secure data. By putting some of the information behind separate firewalls and not keeping credit card information internally, you will lower the risk. There have been huge breaches of security with other "e-tailers." The speed at which criminals can operate enables hackers to disseminate and utilize stolen information in seconds. It's amazing how quickly stolen information can make itself available for sale. An online retailer must be able to provide a 100 percent guarantee on privacy and security. That helps give people confidence. And trust and reliability are cornerstones in online retailing. Without them, it is unlikely that a successful business could be built.

7) Focus on Customer Service

Customer service is probably the most important – and probably the most overlooked – aspect of ensuring a successful customer experience. Anyone getting involved in online retailing should develop an excellent customer service operation. A prominently displayed 1-800 number ensures that our customers can reach us when they need to and reach an actual person trained to listen to both what our customer is saying and suggesting. Many companies outsource this aspect of their business, but for online retailers, it is particularly important to understand the need for, and to take on the expense of, doing this well.

The training of customer service people is also of paramount importance. They have to be able to respond to a customer's needs and not only satisfy them, but ensure that the customer's satisfaction goes beyond a single purchase. The difference between a one-time customer and a life-long customer often boils down to how well you've hired and trained your customer service people. There's no question that this can be expensive but, in the end, the investment is absolutely essential, and worth it. It's always a good problem to have so much traffic that your customer service people are very busy. In an impersonal online environment, that personal contact is of critical importance.

8) Build Credibility Wherever Possible

Credibility is an important issue for many online companies. Because customers can't see in-person, touch, or try on an item they are buying, it is important that they feel comfortable that what they are reading about and seeing a picture of is actually what they are going to get. They have to perceive that there is low risk involved in making the purchase.

There are a number of ways to put customers' minds at ease. The first, and most obvious, is to give them as much accurate information as possible. Product details, customer reviews, ingredients, materials, sizes, etc. – all of this is vital to help make the customer feel comfortable. Another important way of gaining credibility is by offering a full, no-questions-asked return policy. By doing this you can help to ensure that the customer's experience, the most important single factor in successful Internet retailing, is not merely satisfactory but is guaranteed to be so.

Another way to establish credibility with your customers is to deliver excellent service and superior customer relations. As I wrote earlier, a hassle-free return policy, quality guarantees, and vigorous security all signal to your customers that the trust that they invest in you will not be disappointed and that you value their business.

9) Embrace the "Report, Analyze and Refine" Cycle
With so much data at an e-tailers disposal, it is difficult to imagine why so many have been accused of being unresponsive to their customers. Even without a large incoming call center, a web retailer should be set up to analyze aggregated customer behavior on their site. By doing so, they should be able to refine their merchandising strategies and further refine their product offering. This constant and recurring process should not be underestimated. Many of the most successful consumer product companies started out with a market study and a hypothesis on how to capitalize on a particular market need. Many of those companies, through a constant feedback and refining process, ended up identifying other more compelling needs, which propelled them into the sector-leading positions they now enjoy. What cost them millions in focus groups and consumer "taste-tests" can be captured, isolated, and analyzed by a

discerning technical and management team at a far lower cost and with far greater certitude.

Additionally, database analysis, or data mining, can help retailers know with amazing precision most of the details of their customers and their purchasing behavior. The busiest times; the most visited sections; the most profitable sources of first time customers; and the most popular products in rural markets among 35 to 45-year-old married mothers owning an SUV – all of this can be known precisely and in real time. This makes marketing and all corollary initiatives quantifiable. While there is always room for intuition and creativity, the fundamental basis for most decisions can be derived from pure objective data.

This, it can be said without hyperbole, is a revolution in the retail world. And it can only be done online.

10) Personalize the Experience
The reason why security, ultimately, is so important is that online retailers generally collect a substantial amount of data. Using that data to understand your customers and the marketplace is an important key to building a successful online retailing business. Because of the nature of online retailing, companies collect with the agreement of the customer not only their direct personal information, but also their preferences and shopping habits and retailers can use that information to personalize the shopping experience for each individual customer. This invaluable marketing/promotional tool is the true power of Internet retailing and one of the important advantages to conducting business online. Currently the level of personalization attempted by the better online retailers is known as collaborative filtering, in which a retailer can simply present similar products and promotions to a customer based on what that particular customer is looking at or has in his or her shopping cart. "Customers who like product X, also like these products Y and Z" is generally how it's presented. Whether cross-selling products, isolating a specific market

segment, or crafting a promotion for a group of core customers, the degree to which this information can be parsed and used is limited only by the skill and imagination of the online retailer. It is easily one of the most exciting and fast-moving aspects of the online retailing today.

There is only one drawback to this and it is important to recognize. As stated previously, the integrity of a customer's personal information must be paramount in the minds of online retailers. Exploiting data collection for unethical or illegal purposes is obviously not only wrong, but in the end, bad business. The online retailer who doesn't respect their customer, won't have many to deal with.

Some Common Mistakes

We've talked about some of the key factors in creating a successful online retailer and we've also touched on some of the pitfalls specific to starting an online business. Irrational spending was probably the most common mistake made by many of the now defunct online retailers. Today, however, most online businesses have learned that a realistic plan for generating actual profits is the only way to be successful. Exorbitant spending against hypothetical future earnings in order to build a brand has largely gone the way of the dinosaur. Many other problems from the boom years, however, still remain.

Because of the lower cost of initial entry and the Internet frenzy, competition for the consumer's attention and dollar remains fierce. There may be any number of short-term players competing for the same audience. Many of those competitors will eventually fall to the wayside, but new ones are popping up in their place everyday and they are aggressive and smart. Only by planning for the long-term and sticking by that plan can a new online retailer hope to be successful.

Another problem facing online retailers is the lack of face-to-face customer interaction. The Internet is highly impersonal. For many customers, this is the ultimate drawback. Being able to ask for advice and information while looking someone in the eye is the essence of the sales relationship and that is completely lost online. The act of shopping becomes far more passive over the Internet. Customers cannot touch or try-on the product before purchasing it. This is a major setback, particularly in soft goods like apparel, where return rates can be very high. Shipping costs can quickly turn a profitable sale into a net loss.

The Future: Adapting to a Changing Environment
Post Bubble Fall-Out

There's no question that there has been tremendous upheaval in the online retailing sector in the last ten years. From the initial surge of activity and growth in the mid-to-late 90s right up until the bubble burst and beyond, if there's one sector that has experienced change recently, it's the online sector. At the moment, we are still seeing a tremendous amount of fallout from the bubble. Many hundreds of online retailers have closed up shop and the few major players that remain have consolidated the market. In their wake, there are any number of small mom-and-pop operations that continue to have an incremental impact on the online retailing marketplace, but we are still dealing with an incredible disinterest in, and avoidance of, building up online businesses by many corporations and in the marketplace for capital. For some, including MotherNature.com, the volatility of the post-bubble era has played to our advantage, as most of our competitors have fallen by the wayside. We kept our heads low and overhead extremely low, which is one of the main reasons we're still around.

Highlight the Differences

As noted earlier in this chapter, there are many more similarities between online and offline retailing than there are differences. The main differences boil down to speed and information. The information that defines a successful strategy, and the interpretation of that information, arises mainly from the circumstances of the shopping medium. In the digital era, we can know more about the marketplace, our individual customers, and the effectiveness of what we're doing than ever before – and faster than ever before. In the future, these will continue to be the most important factors in online retailing.

Still, some things will never change.

You still have to sell something that people need, or at the very least, perceive that they need. A majority of revenues generally come from a minority of heavy users/shoppers. Building a brand is a slow and expensive process. And a customer's first impression of the store is set within the first few seconds of entering the door. These and so many other factors are the same in retail, no matter where or how you've established your business.

Besides speed and information, however, there is one more aspect of online retailing that is unique and that will likely continue to grow in the future – the level of partnership marketing. There are many thousands of partners all across the Internet working together with online retailers to drive traffic to stores. In exchange for links or promotion, often these companies take a small percentage of any sales that result from their efforts. These cooperative "swarming" techniques allow online retailers to aggressively reach out to targeted partners and spread their message at very little cost to a wide audience of consumers. The key to using this unprecedented level of cooperative connectivity well lies in targeting your partners, or more accurately, their consumer base, effectively. A smart online retailer will identify partners who fit their customer demographic and maximize their promotional activities with these partners. Going forward, I believe that building the right partnerships will be an increasingly important part of online retailing and that the practice of cooperative marketing will continue to grow.

Obviously, there are many other direct differences between offline and online businesses. For instance, capital spending on technology is much higher in online businesses. But, for the most part, despite these obvious differences, the future will show that the more retailing changes, the more it stays the same. Online retailing is merely the latest twist on an old song.

An Informed Customer is a Better Customer

One result of the growth of online retailing is that customers are now more informed than ever about not only the products they are interested in, but also the processes by which those products may be purchased. In short, online retailing enables individuals to be more proactive, and it forces retailers to deal with people on an individual level rather than by broad trends. Some of our largest and most profitable customers insist upon individualized service. That's one of the strengths of the Internet and it's something that we've gone to great lengths to address. Most consumers don't realize that they have great leverage in having stores cater to them. Offline, when you walk into a store, in the United States especially, people are accustomed to paying the price that's advertised and not being part of the decision-making process. Online shopping is a definite departure from what we're used to and almost trained to do as consumers. At the moment, 98 percent of all retail purchasing is done offline; but as this number shrinks, I think we will see empowered customers using their clout to seek out the best deals both in the online and offline retail world.

The Future

This last year may not necessarily be indicative of where the industry is going, but it's clear that the online retailing component is one of the brighter spots in retail. That was evident especially over the last holiday season, when online retailing was experiencing 30 to 50 percent jumps in revenue, while retailing as a whole was seeing a contraction across most sectors. The online component makes too much sense for every company not to have an online strategy. It's a phenomenally powerful channel – more powerful than any other single channel, in my opinion. But it has its place. It will be an important channel, and will make in-roads, but it's not going to replace the offline retail experience anytime soon.

Going forward, we'll continue to see further consolidation by the major players and continued growth for online retailing, particularly in certain areas like books and music, but also as a whole. In certain industries (easy-to-ship or easy-to-download items such as software, music, books) there will be more movement than others, but in most it will assume the role of "one of several" important distribution channels all of which should work well together.

Everyday, thousands of new users are coming online. The youngest generations, composed of the children of the baby boomers, are coming of age in an era where shopping on the Internet is as natural as going to the corner store for a quart of milk. Their comfort level and familiarity with online shopping as they become teenagers and young adults virtually ensures continued growth for online retailing. But there are real concerns ahead as well. Increasing competition and consolidation, and other factors, like efforts to impose a sales tax on online purchases, could impact estimates of future growth. Nevertheless, I am optimistic about the future and in the years ahead, we will undoubtedly see online retailing become an ever more important part of the overall retail landscape.

Mr. Anderson is serial entrepreneur with significant experience in early-stage company development. His background includes over twelve years focused on the operation, financing and building of early-stage businesses and turnaround situations. In the past 5 years, he has acquired, managed and sold several online consumer product and service companies. Previously, he was a founding principal of ReNewal Realty, LLC, a company dedicated to the acquisition and redevelopment of environmentally contaminated retail properties ("Brownfields"). He was also a founding principal of AFW Asset Management, a merchant banking firm specializing in technology investments. He has also been a guest lecturer at Pace University on environmental finance and socially responsible investing. He graduated from Cornell University.

Knowing Your Business...

Means Knowing Your Customer, First

Steven G. Puett

Las Vegas Golf & Tennis
President and Chief Executive Officer

Establishing Customer Relationships

While some may view the successful delivery of product to market as a relatively simple process from point A (the vendor or manufacturer) to point B (the retailer), it is certainly much broader than that. Ultimate and continuous success must encompass the full supply chain, from mutually beneficial supplier partnerships, efficient and effective distribution of materials, quality of the product delivered, proper merchandising, and last but certainly not least, acquisition by the consumer. Delivery of product to market does not stop with merchandising on the retailers' shelf; rather, the definition of "market" must include the final and most important step – the consumer purchase. Clearly the most important link in the art of retail, if it had to be defined by one key aspect, is taking care of the customer. You can carry the right product mix, provide the best merchandising, and operate at the highest possible margins, but if customers don't feel compelled to shop at your store and buy the products you carry, you're not going to be successful. As a specialty retailer with a very defined customer base, as opposed to a mass merchant with its broad base of customers, this becomes even more important.

Las Vegas Golf & Tennis is a specialty retailer in the sporting goods industry. In other words, we do not carry a broad line of products outside of our specific market. Everything we do is related to golf and tennis – equipment, apparel, footwear, and various accessories. Because of that, the staff in our stores is highly knowledgeable about those products and always available to assist customers with their questions or with decisions they have to make.

When someone walks into one of our facilities it is important to us that we know they are getting the best possible service, and hopefully with a sale, also the best equipment to address their needs and wants. To do so requires probing that customer with a number of questions to better understand their game and skill level. We want to establish a level of knowledge about the customer and then use our knowledge of the various products available to best fit their game. No one should have an interest or desire in making the "quick sell." Successful specialty retailers will strive for a long-term relationship with their customers rather than a one-time sale.

Upon initially entering the store, our staff and franchisees have been trained to first observe something about the customer. We let them walk around for a few minutes and see what they are looking at and then walk up and simply establish a conversation. NEVER approach a customer to ask, "How can I help you?" or "Can I help you find anything?" While most would find those questions to be quite appropriate and sincere, the reality is that after asking either question nine times out of ten the customer will respond by saying, "No thank you, I'm just browsing" or something similar. The problem with these types of introductory questions is that customers hear them at most places they shop, and therefore have become conditioned to interpreting the question to actually mean "how can I help sell you something today?" The same is true in respect to handing a customer your business card and telling them to ask for you if they return to make a purchase. My belief has always been that if a salesperson is helpful, knowledgeable, and does their job correctly, then the customer will ask them for their business card. Why would a customer want to start all over explaining what they are looking for with another salesperson if you have already established a positive relationship? You just don't approach a customer and give them the impression that you are trying to sell them something. You approach the customer and establish a conversation about golf, or tennis, or maybe even the latest TV show. We've found that most customers really like to talk about their golf game, especially if they happen to have had a good round recently or perhaps even just made a couple of good shots that day. Once you've established a conversation and developed a comfortable relationship with the customer, their perception is that you didn't approach them to make a sale but rather because you care about them personally and have some knowledge that will be helpful with their decision. That is when you start your probing. We probably spend much more time with our customers – whether we make a sale or not – than a typical retail store does.

What Makes a Good Salesperson?

In terms of finding employees, it is the quality and attitude of the person that are most important. An intelligent person can learn certain specifics about any industry. For example, if an individual receives the proper training they can learn how to correctly fit someone to a set of golf clubs. It certainly helps if you already play, because you're more familiar with some of the terminology and will learn that much quicker. On the other hand, I'm not sure you can always train someone how to help a customer. I believe some people are innately, or have become so through their life experiences, more considerate and perceptive than others. You can however teach the process, and that is why to us, for example, probing is so important. Sometimes retailers and people in the sales business get too caught up in selling and forget about servicing!

When selling you want to focus on "assets" (those things that have value to your customer) as opposed to "attributes" (any of potentially numerous features of a given product). Take, for example, a customer looking for a small cup. A knowledgeable salesperson can explain all the dynamics of a Styrofoam cup (lightweight, disposable, inexpensive, keeps hot things hot and cold things cold, etc.) but a good salesperson would first ask what the cup is going to be used for – in this case, watering small plants in the office. What we try to do is always ask the probing questions first, such as "What is your typical ball flight?" or "What is it about your game that you're trying to improve?" Once we have enough understanding of a specific customer, then we can focus on those products that will help enhance their game and provide them with the best options that specifically address their needs and wants. Otherwise you are just talking to them about features and attributes that may have no relevance to them as a customer and the intended purchase or use of the item.

The other aspect that we also try to focus on is add-ons. I think in many ways add-ons, perhaps because of the fast-food industry, have developed a less than favorable reputation. Granted if you don't ask you are likely not going to get the sale, but it needs to be more sincere than "Do you want fries with that order?" In our case, if you don't ask, you can actually alienate a customer. There are a number of items we sell that go hand in hand with other products. For example, selling a set of clubs to a beginning golfer and not asking if they also need a putter. If offering add-ons is done sincerely, it is helpful. Again, it should be relative to what the customer needs.

Lastly, there needs to be some type of mechanism in place to ensure salespeople are following the processes and using the tools provided to them. One simple way of doing this is employing Secret Shoppers. This is a relatively low cost service that can provide significant feedback from the customer's perspective. Establish the criteria you want to be monitored (e.g., was I greeted when I entered the store, what was the salesperson's introductory comment, was the salesperson helpful, knowledgeable, etc.) and then share the results. You may even want to implement some type of incentive plan for those who achieve the best results.

Separating Yourself from Your Competition

Retail is very relationship driven and because our industry, at least for hard goods, is also largely a commodity-driven industry, we have to focus on how we differentiate ourselves from our competitors if we are essentially selling many of the same items at the same prices. You can walk into any golf or tennis shop and buy the same driver, the same set of irons, or the same tennis racquet for essentially the same price. For the most part, you can get it anywhere you want to go within this industry. So the question then is how do we differentiate ourselves?

A big part of that process, as previously referenced, is establishing relationships with our customers. Know them on a first and last name basis. Know what their last significant purchase was. Know if they have been pleased with that purchase. Second, we have to make sure we are knowledgeable about the products that we carry. If customers have questions, we provide them answers. If we don't have the answers, we certainly know where to find the answers and can get back to them. Third, we can differentiate ourselves with a broader product mix and better selection in other areas, such as apparel and accessories. These things are extremely important in our business because absent the customer relationship, the product knowledge, and the larger selection of certain items, there's no compelling reason for a customer not to buy from a mass merchant or off the Internet.

Keeping customers happy pays off in more ways than just keeping them loyal to your store. Positive customer comments are the least expensive and yet the most effective type of advertising a retailer can generate; it's a fairly well-known principle that acquiring a new customer generally costs five times more than keeping the one you already have. Conversely, dissatisfied customers can very quickly spread their negative comments to others as well – possibly preventing them from ever becoming customers. Another general rule of thumb is that customers will share their negative experiences on average to nine other people, more often than their positive experiences. Because golf and tennis are both highly social activities, it is even more likely that these experiences will be shared.

Another way we separate ourselves from our competitors is with our Point of Sale system, which allows us to maintain a preferred customer list. The system keeps a record of all the purchases made by our customers so it is not necessary for them to keep copies of their receipts. If they need to send a product back under warranty, we have proof of purchase because it is documented under their name. If they need to make a return or an exchange, they don't need the receipt; they can just come in and we'll look up the purchase in the database. It can also be helpful when an individual is buying a gift for someone else. A good example would be when a wife comes in and asks for help in buying her husband a new pair of golf shoes but can't recall what size he wears. We can check the database and find out what size he bought the last time he purchased a pair of shoes. Another common occurrence is when a group of employees is trying to buy a parting gift for an associate who is retiring. They may not know where to start but we can offer a number of recommendations based on that individual's purchasing history, e.g., possibly a new fairway wood to match the driver that was purchased a few months earlier. The system is an extremely valuable tool for us and our customers are just amazed that they are able to walk in without a receipt and exchange something. We don't sell our customer database. It is not for marketing purposes. The only other primary use is to notify our customers if we are having a sale.

Goals and Vision

First, it is important to understand the differences between long-term and short-term objectives. Long-term goals are the vision of what you are striving to become. They are always out there and are not something you want to change very often. As such, they are an integral part of your business strategy and define who you want to become and how long the process may take. Everything that every employee within the business is striving for and working on each day should support that longer-term vision.

Our vision is that we want to be the most successful sporting goods franchise company in the industry. Success to us does not mean that we are the largest or the fastest growing; those are parameters resulting from other accomplishments. Success to us means that once we open a location, we want that location to hit or exceed certain benchmarks that will ensure its success, whether it is a corporate location or a franchise location. As long as we achieve that specific objective, the other two (i.e., largest and fastest) should happen consequently. That is, if we are one of the most successful companies in terms of operating profitable locations, then ultimately we should become one of the fastest growing and one of the largest, as opposed to an entity that may open twenty locations but two or three years down the road half of them have failed. That is not the model we want to follow.

We also have established some simple but highly relevant key principles that guide us in support of our vision. They are as follows:

If it's the Right Decision for the Customer…It's the Right Decision for Las Vegas Golf & Tennis
Honesty, Respect and Integrity in All Business and Personal Dealings
Work as a Team and Provide Unequaled Support
Use Common Sense and Learn From Mistakes
Strive for Continuous Improvement in All Aspects of Our Business
If it's the Right Thing to Do… Do It Now!

Regarding short-term objectives, I learned a long time ago that all goals must meet the criteria of being SMART. That is, they must be: Specific, Measurable, Achievable, Relevant, and Trackable.

One other key aspect of goals is that they need to be visible. If you're traveling uncharted territory, how do you know if you're heading the right direction without occasionally checking the roadmap? There are many people who spend an exorbitant amount of time establishing clearly defined objectives only to file them away. Then at the end of the year, or some infrequent basis, they decide to pull them out to see how they are doing. If you keep them visible – tracked and measured on a more frequent basis – you know if you are on target or not, and whether or not changes need to be made. There should not be any surprises relevant to hitting your objectives.

There are, however, typically a couple of different ways to hit a target: (1) Ready, Aim, Aim, Aim... and then Fire or (2) Ready, Aim... Fire, Fire, Fire. While both can get you the same end result, the first scenario is usually more efficient while the second is more effective. You have to decide which the better process is given the specific circumstances. Home runs are great but sometimes a base hit is all you need.

Financial Measures

Generating sales is largely driven by customer service, product mix, merchandising and advertising – and certainly you have to have a good location to begin with. One of the key performance indicators for any retailer is sales growth versus prior year. Other good benchmarks are sales per square foot, and sales per work hour or payroll dollar. Obviously you can spend a lot of money on advertising or run numerous sales promotions to increase sales, but you need to make sure the cash flow being generated is enough to justify the expense.

There are also numerous measurements relative to the operating aspects of the store (e.g., inventory turns and profit margin). Rather than looking at each store as the basic unit in terms of its operating parameters, we prefer to evaluate each specific business segment individually. These segments are the hard goods business, the apparel business, the footwear business, the accessory business, and the ball business. Each segment has extremely different parameters that will determine whether it is a successful business or not. Profit margins, inventory turns, carrying costs, space requirements, vendor terms, etc., can vary significantly from one business segment to the other. To evaluate the store as a whole rather than looking at each specific business will not allow for optimum performance. You have to track each one independently and make sure that each segment is achieving its objectives. If you can do that, even if one segment may be under performing due to weather or other known factors, you are still going to have a successful operation. We not only want to ensure that a store is profitable and hitting its sales targets, we want to optimize the profitability of each specific business segment for that location. Ultimately, we want each business unit and each location to reach their maximum potential.

Changes and Trends

In business you have to be prepared for change, and you should not only accept it but preferably be in a continuous race with it – i.e., not too far ahead and not too far behind but comfortably in stride. It is always beneficial to recognize change as a business opportunity (proactive preparation) as opposed to modifying your business to fit the new environment (reactive restoration). In the case of most retailers, there has been a significant change from operating a traditional brick-and-mortar retail business to establishing and/or competing with internet businesses. The success of either is still largely and solely dependent upon whether or not you take care of your customers. It doesn't matter if you are brick-and-mortar or electronic. As the saying goes "change is inevitable except from vending machines." The one constant remaining, however, is that the primary focus for all retailers is taking care of the customer. We exist for one reason, and that is to fulfill the needs and/or wants of the people who visit our stores or websites.

The retailing industry has also seen a shift toward the big-box or mega store. Wal-Mart has probably been the most successful. Because of the company's large distribution channel, it is certainly within reason that Wal-Mart could get into any business segment they choose. People walk into those facilities on a very frequent basis. Not because they have needs and wants, but because they have requirements: clothing, food, school supplies, etc. They have a built-in customer base every day and have done a tremendous job of expanding the product lines that they carry. At some point in the future they could decide to become more heavily involved in the sporting goods business. The change at that point to the industry won't have as much of an impact on us as a specialty retailer as it will on perhaps the mass merchant sporting goods stores – the reason being that I would categorize a mass merchant sporting goods store as more similar to a Wal-Mart. Because of the broad product lines they carry and the size of their operations, they aren't typically as proficient relative to customer service. That is not meant to imply that they are not courteous and helpful. Wal-Mart has a very good reputation compared to other mass merchants, but would likely fall short in the product knowledge category if compared to most specialty retailers. Our goal is to make sure that we are the most knowledgeable about the products we sell. With everything else being equal, customers prefer shopping at a specialty store because they can get that extra value.

Within the last couple of years there has been a proliferation and an abundance of new products that have been introduced that, in my opinion, were not necessarily needed. Too many manufacturers are trying to focus on bringing out the latest and greatest, and they are not giving their existing product lines the opportunity to really grow and thrive. Consumers have become well aware of this. They know that if they wait three to six months they can probably pay $100 less for the new hot driver that just hit the market. This has a significant negative impact on the industry as a whole, and even more so during a soft spending economy. There is an oversupply of equipment and golf balls because the manufacturers are changing product lines too often. As a result, probably one of the largest markets right now is the used club business. Again, that is damaging the sales of new equipment. I think the industry needs to slow down the introduction of equipment just for the sake of having new product. There's no such thing as a cash cow anymore because a product's life cycle has been cut too short.

Challenges and Rewards of Retail

This is a growing industry. The golf industry specifically has seen some significant growth relative to the number of participants in the past decade, and one of the few sports to receive more lucrative TV broadcasting agreements in the past few years. With a larger percentage of females and juniors taking up the sport, and baby boomers just beginning to hit the retirement age (which provides more leisure time), it has a very promising future. People have been playing golf for centuries and there is no reason for that not to continue. I think the more attractive we can make it, perhaps a little less time consuming, and the less costly we can make it, the easier it becomes for people to pick up the game and continue to enjoy it.

Tennis also has a promising future. The phenomena of the Williams sisters are unmatched in history, and ladies' tennis continues to gain increased media exposure. Men's tennis also shows promise with the emergence of Andy Roddick and other young talent ready to step in and fill the void as Sampras and Agassi approach retirement.

Both golf and tennis are sports one can start to play at an early age and continue to enjoy for a lifetime. They're both also beneficial in the aspect that you don't need ten other players in order to play the game. You can certainly go out and play golf by yourself. There are many attributes about this industry that are extremely attractive. However, that is not to say the industry is without its challenges.

We have many prospects that are interested in getting into the business and running a franchise, but we have to make sure they stay focused on the business. For people who are truly golf and tennis enthusiasts and love getting out and playing themselves, there are many nice perks that can come with the business, but they can't lose sight of the fact that it is still a business nonetheless. It still runs on profitability. If you lose track of that because you are out taking advantage of some of the perks, you may reach the point where you no longer have a business to operate.

Generally, in running our stores, one of the biggest issues is managing inventory. We do not operate on extremely high margins. Certainly we are above the grocery industry, but we are typically below other sporting goods industries. That means you really have to pay attention to managing your cash flow in that you are putting your dollars into inventory that preferably is "coming in and going out the door" rather than "coming in and sitting on the floor."

The most exciting part of retail is that it is a fun business. When customers walk into or out of a golf and tennis store, they usually have a smile on their face, especially if we are doing our job correctly. That's the way it should be. That makes it fun to come to work each day.

Steve Puett is the President and CEO of Las Vegas Golf & Tennis, a specialty retailer and international franchise operation in the sporting goods industry. Prior to this position Mr. Puett had been a successful franchisee of Las Vegas Golf & Tennis for a number of years, and was voted to serve on the advisory board of Las Vegas Golf & Tennis by *other franchisees to best represent their interests. Previously, Mr. Puett served as Vice-President of Logistics for Pameco Corporation, a 350 branch, $500 million wholesaler of HVAC and refrigeration equipment and supplies. Mr. Puett has also directed the operations for 7,500 retail stores in the automotive after-market retail business, and formerly held numerous management positions in supply chain, information systems, and quality control with The Dow Chemical Company. Mr. Puett received a BS in Business Administration from the University of Tennessee, Knoxville.*

The Retailer as Artist

Jeffrey W. Griffiths

Electronics Boutique Holdings Corp.
President and Chief Executive Officer

The Making of a Retail Masterpiece

Operating a successful retail store is indeed an art form. And, just as art encompasses a spectrum of different mediums and techniques, retailing spans a wide variety of industries and operating formats. As a result, the challenges and advantages faced by different retailers can vary dramatically, and the ways in which each retailer needs to meet its individual challenges can be equally diverse.

That said, there are certain retailing tenets that can help spell success for every retailer in every industry, from the smallest "Mom and Pop" convenience store to the largest international department store chain. Among other things, these tenets include: cultivating and projecting a "signature style," leveraging the opportunities inherent in reviewing daily performance numbers, knowing and understanding your audience, keeping pace with changes in the marketplace, and continuously planning for the future.

In the following chapter, I'll outline my thoughts on each of these points, and then I'll take a look at the "big picture" of my particular industry – video game hardware and software, PC entertainment software, and accessories – and the unique challenges and opportunities that it holds. I'll conclude by offering some insight into my personal vision on management techniques and retailing strategies.

The Importance of Cultivating a Signature Style

The artists that rise to fame are those that are able to set themselves apart in a meaningful way. They often accomplish this feat by creating a distinctive look for their masterpieces – one that appeals to the tastes of consumers and cannot easily be replicated. This "signature style" defines their body of work and enables them to create a loyal following of admirers.

Retailing is much the same. Successful retailers create a loyal following of customers by developing and maintaining certain hallmarks – from an unusual store format, to a unique set of special services, to a clearly defined shopping atmosphere – that are tough to find elsewhere. By cultivating these characteristics, good retailers build awareness of their brand and help to make sure that consumers associate that brand with a "personality" that will draw them in to shop again and again.

As a result, creating a good "signature style" is a crucial path to retailing success. At the same time, it's one of the biggest challenges that retailers face. In order to remain exciting to customers, we must be constantly changing what we offer, continually adjusting our product and service selections and regularly enhancing our image, all while retaining the core characteristics that set us apart. These challenges are even more difficult because it's virtually impossible for a retailer to keep its "secrets of success" obvious to consumers yet hidden from competitors. As a result, good ideas are relatively easy for others to analyze and copy, requiring us to reach over and over for new ways to differentiate ourselves. Staying in front of this cycle requires tenacity, stamina and creativity. But doing so consistently often translates to long-term rewards.

The Value of Leveraging Daily Performance Numbers

One of the most exciting advantages retailers have in pursuing these endeavors is that we can see the results of our efforts in "real-time." Since we have daily sales, we have the opportunity to look at how every store is performing on a daily basis, both in relation to its individual targets and in contrast to how it did last year. We can also rapidly gauge consumer reaction to new products, we can regularly evaluate how well all of our products are selling, and we can instantly assess consumer reaction to our marketing efforts.

The immediacy of this feedback affords a retailer several valuable advantages. First, we can see generally see pretty quickly if things are going according to plan, instead of having to wait until the end of each quarter when it's often too late to react effectively. If things are going well, we get instant gratification, and we are positioned to respond quickly to new opportunities – by making our plans more ambitious or by replicating them in other areas. If things are falling short, we can make adjustments, assess reaction to those, and continue this process until we get the results that we want. Being so close to the "outcome" end of the business, retailers have the flexibility to make rapid changes in any part of their operation that can help them to adapt to changes in the environment.

Another advantage to the immediacy aspect of retailing is that it tends to generate a level of energy that serves as a driver for greater success. In essence, seeing the hard numbers on a daily basis gives retailers something concrete to look forward to every single day. This energy is further enhanced in categories that are subject to rapid change, as is the case with the category of product that we sell – video games and PC games. Since the growth of these industries is driven by advances in technology, new games are continually being released, and the quality of these games is better all the time. As a result, we operate in a really exciting product category that actually has the ability to build its own momentum.

The Necessity of Knowing Your Audience

There's an old saying that beauty is in the eye of the beholder, and this is certainly true in the art world. High-demand art styles run from the avant-garde to the classical, and touch everything in between. To be a commercial success, an artist needs to match his or her style with an audience who appreciates it, and create works that satisfy that group's aesthetic preferences.

Retail offers a clear parallel. In fact, if I could single out only one rule for retailers to apply, it would be this: Know your customer. It's a rule I constantly employ myself, and one I promote continuously by reminding all of my employees to keep the customer in mind. And, the reality is, it's a point that continues to grow in importance. Today, the competitive field is made up of numerous good retailers, many of whom are highly efficient. The field is always getting stronger, and as it does, consumers have many good choices of places to shop. In addition, the widespread use of the Internet has enabled consumers to become much better informed than they were in the past. They know they have numerous choices of where to get the products they want, where to go for the best prices and where to get the services they desire. To compete, we retailers have to instill confidence in every customer that walks through our doors. The best way to do this is to know our customers intimately – to understand precisely what they want so we can provide it for them on a consistent basis.

And, it should come as no surprise that it's often the obvious little things that are most important to customers. They want us to offer solid services and fair prices. They want us to provide a good shopping experience that is consistent with each visit to each location. They want us to be efficient, so that the products they want are not only available but also easy for them to find. They want us to be fair, standing behind the products we sell with satisfaction guarantees. If we fail in any of these areas on just one occasion, a customer may leave our store and never return. In short, we don't choose the customer; the customer chooses us, and for them to continually do so, we need to make every experience a good experience.

The Significance of Keeping Pace with the Times

Retail is anything but a static art form. In fact, change continues to accelerate the transformation of the retail industry at an unprecedented pace. Technology keeps improving, and along with it, the ability to share and disseminate information is exploding. In retailing, this has spawned an increasingly competitive marketplace where only the strongest survive. Indeed, to be able to grow in retailing today, you must be able to expand. In so doing, many current "up-and-coming" retailers are taking business away from less efficient retailers. In the end, the consumer benefits through access to a better selection of products, better store in-stock positions and better pricing.

In this environment, retailers must constantly improve, regardless of how good they already are – even being number one in the market doesn't count for very long unless you keep driving improvements. A good goal to have is to be better every year in as many areas a possible, from pricing to product allocation, store in-stock positions, customer service and store construction. The bottom line is that if you don't improve every year, you'll lose business to someone else who did. And the range of issues to improve is also growing. Today's consumers have more choices than ever before, and they're more intelligent and better informed. Years ago, the average consumer was dependent on store salespeople to provide product education; now, armed with in-depth product information gleaned from the Internet, consumers walk into stores with a wealth of knowledge and higher service expectations. As a result, in many cases the role of the salesperson has shifted from providing product knowledge to creating an easy, value-added shopping experience. This has raised the bar for retailers, and today, when a customer comes to our stores to buy a product, they expect it to be in stock, easily accessible and competitively priced. If it's not, they know exactly where to go to buy it from someone else who will meet these needs.

While keeping pace with ever-growing consumer demands seems daunting, retailers have an important tool at their disposal to help them to meet these demands – technology. It always impresses me how incredibly efficient most retailers have become in recent years. We've eliminated the scores of people we needed to manage back-room functions 30 years ago, replacing them with cutting-edge computer systems that network far-flung stores, manage global inventory systems, control shrink, and process merchandise through distribution centers faster and cheaper than we ever thought possible. All of this enables today's retailers to provide consumers with products that have more value at lower prices.

To succeed in the future, we must continue to follow this trend. We need to develop and leverage increasingly advanced technological systems that improve the ways we manage our products, and that link our systems with those of our suppliers so that we both have better forecasting tools.

The Advantages of Sketching Out the Future

Of course, planning for the future encompasses much more than simply planning to meet growing customer service needs. One of the biggest challenges that any retailer has is developing a viable long-term business plan that dovetails with the realities of the marketplace. In the soft economic environment that we have experienced in recent years, this is an even more difficult task than it was in the past. Nonetheless, retailers who set clear targets that are based on anticipated opportunities in the marketplace and their own potential as a business are at a distinct advantage over those who focus only on the near term. Through a solid long-range plan, retailers can "steer their course" more effectively, and they can develop a concrete method for measuring their progress – all of which serves as an incentive for management to continue to excel.

I believe that at minimum, retailers should set obvious financial goals for each year, such as the projected amount of increases in sales, earnings per share, comparable store sales, and new store openings. These are the four main financial goals that we look at in our company. Using them as a basis, we drill down a little bit to set more long-term objectives. For example, we look at each market that we're in, as well as potential new markets, and we try to select the ones that offer the greatest long-term growth opportunities.

Looking at the Big Picture

As I said at the opening of this chapter, retailing spans a wide variety of industries and operating formats, which together create a unique set of challenges and advantages for every retailer in business. A look at the "big picture" for our company, Electronics Boutique, provides a perfect example. As a leading global retailer that is exclusively dedicated to selling video game hardware and software, PC entertainment software, and accessories, we operate in a particularly fast-paced industry in which new games are launched every week. This factor affords us the exceptional benefit of working in an exciting, energetic marketplace where fresh merchandise continuously attracts customers in to make new purchases. At the same time, our industry holds intense challenges for us that not all retailers face to the same degree. One of these is the constant need for extremely accurate merchandise planning.

Typically, after each new title is released, it enjoys a peak selling period for the next week or two. After that, sales for that game generally taper off, and the next new game released drives sales for the following week or two. The nature of this business is, therefore, somewhat like that of other trend-driven industries like fashion, music or movies. It requires us to go through a careful planning process with every game we purchase through which we try to forecast the level of demand we anticipate so we can purchase a compatible quantity. We measure our success by how closely our actual sales align with our targets. If we have good sell-through of a game early on – one that matches our sales expectations – then we consider the game and our allocation of it to be a success. This is true regardless of the quantity that we sell. For example, if we sell 1,000 pieces of a product that we buy 1,100 of, we consider it a highly successful product, but if we sell 100,000 pieces of a product that we purchase 200,000 of, we don't consider it successful.

The need to gauge change in the marketplace also extends to a longer time horizon. Every four or five years a new generation of console systems comes along, requiring us to help both the market and consumers transition from one platform to another. As part of this cycle, we generally experience slower sales as old systems begin to be phased out, making certain periods more challenging from a top-line sales standpoint. While these are major challenges, we've really thrived on them. Five or six years ago, PC games and PC software were a significant percentage of our business; now much of the PC business has gone, having been consolidated into Microsoft Office and Windows, which are now sold with every PC. Likewise, all the reference products that we used to sell have been completely eliminated, having been made available via the Internet. Meanwhile, our business has grown, as we've leveraged new hardware and software cycles to shift our business mix to the games market and drive sales. Changes like these are tough to adapt to, but I think that our regular exposure to them in this industry ultimately makes us resilient retailers that are well-equipped to adapt to a dynamic market environment.

As is the case with other trend-driven retailers, our swiftly changing product mix demands that we always keep our finger on the pulse of the market so that we can consistently make sound purchasing decisions. And at our company, we must do it on a broad scale. To serve the needs of our customer base as well as we can, we've adopted a "superstore" format, through which we sell an exceptionally wide selection of products that relate to a single, narrow category – in our case, video games – and we conduct our business through an extensive retail network that includes more than 1,200 retail stores in the United States and abroad, as well as a catalog and an e-commerce site. The vast majority of our business is done through our stores, a factor that yields several benefits for our company. One of these is that we can develop a proven system and then apply it almost universally. For the most part, we utilize the same strategy for opening and managing each of our stores, we apply the same business plan to all of our stores, and we sell a very similar product mix in each location. We have systems that can make adjustments to the product mix if a particular store or regional market demonstrates a tendency to be somewhat different from the overall mix.

While our stores definitely leverage the advantages of shared plans and efficiencies, they are all run according to their individual profiles. Every store manager is encouraged to achieve a sales and profit plan and an inventory management plan that is unique to that location. We have a bonus structure for our managers, as well as various other incentives for our sales associates and part-time associates. We tie all of these incentives in with the individual store's goals and, ultimately, with our company's overall financial and operating objectives, including sales volume, bottom line and inventory shrink control.

Another major challenge that we face in our industry is that we're dependent upon third-party companies to provide us with a steady flow of appealing products. Unlike a bakery that bakes bread every day and sells it, we don't create the products we sell, and, therefore, we rely on our vendor partners to provide games and consoles that our customers will want to buy. To some extent, this impacts our ability to develop a long-term business plan. We manage this issue by reviewing intensive market research that enables us to create and evolve our business plan from one year to the next. For example, we look at industry trends and analyze market data to formulate predictions on the industry growth rate for upcoming years. We review our current market share position to determine our sales potential for the following year, and from that we decide how many stores we think we will open. Then we look at our existing store base to identify where we should locate new stores so that we can enter promising new markets and increase our penetration of established markets.

Of course, managing our growth presents another challenge – a positive one that all healthy companies face. At the core of this is finding the right employees for our stores. We open an average of 300 stores per year, and we need to find good, enthusiastic staff members for all those stores. In addition, we have a certain amount of turnover in our existing stores that requires us to seek new employees on a fairly regular basis. We place a high priority on having sales associates who are passionate about games and highly knowledgeable about our products. We've found that one of the best resources for employees with these qualifications is our customer base.

Most of our customers love games and want to be associated with them. They visit our stores frequently and talk to our existing employees about our products. In the course of this, they gain an understanding of our store work environment, and they are drawn to the fact that our employees get product discounts, have access to new games before they come out and get opportunities to attend trade shows. Ultimately, some of these customers end up becoming employees, and they help to foster our deep commitment to the industry. We also work hard to retain our employees, and that is made easier by the fact that our ongoing growth generates significant opportunities for advancement. Good sales associates can quickly become store managers, store managers can become district managers, and so on, meaning that we provide our employees with the possibility for turning a hobby into a solid career opportunity.

Another challenge for our company – and for businesses across many industries – is continuing to grow in today's soft economy. Fortunately for us, our industry is fairly resistant to economic dips. Games are highly popular at-home entertainment products that are relatively inexpensive. Our target customer – a male in his teens to mid-30s – tends to have a relatively stable amount of disposable income, and considers gaming a fairly high priority. We've found that the characteristics of our target customer are incredibly strong and stable, making them more important than the impact of macro-economic concerns.

The Benefits of Managing as a Team

We handle all of the challenges that we face by working as a team – a factor that I firmly believe is one of the keys to successful retailing. I strongly advocate sharing information with employees, explaining the company's vision and strategy, outlining our plans, and then giving our people the tools necessary to perform their jobs in a way that fulfills those goals. We have a senior management group that is involved in all major strategic decisions and most operational decisions. We have weekly operating committee meetings in which each department has the opportunity to present any issues they have, discuss how they're performing, and get feedback from other departments. All in all, it's a very open, team-oriented atmosphere where everyone has a chance to contribute, and everyone is inspired to have confidence in our company. We have a very low turnover in middle management and senior management, and I think that's a reflection on that.

As CEO, I believe that my primary roles are to keep my finger on two things. One is acting as the spokesperson to the shareholders and the analysts – sharing our vision with them and keeping them informed of our progress and our plans. The other is managing and balancing our short-term goals with our long-term goals. I view our short-term goals as the quarterly goals that we manage as part of our responsibility as a public company. Our long-term goal is to ensure that our company will be able to continue to grow and prosper in the years ahead. One of my core priorities is to make sure that we strike a proper balance in focusing on all of these needs so that neither of them is neglected.

Indeed, my primary objective is to ensure that the company is able to grow, so that it will be more prosperous five or ten years from now. I think that the clearest sign of a successful retailer is the ability to continue to grow consistently over a long period of time while making the company exciting and appealing to the consumer. One of the ways that we are working to do this is by seizing the opportunity to be a global retailer and expand internationally. We want people to go anywhere in the world, see our brand and get the same kind of commitment to service, inventory, and pricing that they get here in the United States.

So, how does one engage in the art of retailing? In short, you have to set a tone that puts the customer first. You need to send a clear message throughout your organization that reinforces to your employees that understanding and taking care of customers is of paramount importance. You have to make sure that products are in stock when customers want them, that your prices are competitive, and that you have customer-friendly policies. You need to keep up with changes in the marketplace so that you can meet the dynamic expectations of consumers. You have to hire people who like your business and the product you sell, and you need to cultivate their commitment by sharing your business vision with them and by creating opportunities for advancement. At the end of the day, you'll be able to confirm that the customer is getting a good experience by seeing in your organization the hallmarks of a retail "masterpiece" – escalating sales, a growing customer base, and sustained success.

Jeffrey Griffiths has served as President and CEO of Electronics Boutique and a Class I Director since June 2001. Mr. Griffiths served as Electronics Boutique's Senior Vice President of Merchandising and Distribution from March 1998 to June 2001. Mr. Griffiths served as Senior Vice President of Merchandising and Distribution of Electronics Boutique's predecessor from March 1996. From March 1987 to February 1996, Mr. Griffiths served as Vice President of Merchandising of Electronics Boutique's predecessor and, from April 1984 to February 1987, he served as the Merchandise Manager of Electronics Boutique's predecessor. Mr. Griffiths earned a B.A. degree in History from Albright College and an M.B.A. degree from Temple University. Mr. Griffiths serves on the Board of Directors of the Interactive Entertainment Merchants Association.

Reaching the Customer

Ken Walker
Meineke Car Care Center, Inc.
President & CEO

In 2002, Meineke celebrated its 30th year as an automotive repair franchise chain. Since its founder Sam Meineke sold the first franchise in Houston, Texas, the business has grown to nearly 900 locations in the US, Canada, Central and South America. How do we continue to attract consumers year after year in a highly competitive market? We focus on an evolving brand image, efficient use of advertising dollars, and fostering trust between Meineke customers and staff.

Meineke is a service retailer, as opposed to a merchandising retailer. Historically, consumers came to Meineke because they had a problem – their muffler fell off or their brakes squealed – and Meineke was there to fix it. These were not discretionary purchases, but rather "grudge" purchases. Like a visit to the dentist, automotive repair was not something a consumer looked forward to – they simply hoped to have the experience over as quickly and painlessly as possible, and preferred not to see the repairman any more often than absolutely necessary.

In the early days of our business, this relationship worked well for both sides. Consumers had their vehicles repaired quickly and inexpensively, and Meineke built a reputation as the number one discount exhaust repair chain in the country. But, as with most industries, technology changed. In 1983, manufacturers began converting cars' exhaust systems from cold-rolled steel to stainless steel and, by 1996, every new vehicle carried a stainless steel muffler. That conversion changed the life span of a muffler from roughly three years to ten years or more. While that change was happy news to most consumers, the impact on Meineke's repeat business would have been staggering.

Our first challenge was to expand our product offering. Over the past several years, Meineke has selectively added items to its service menu, first playing to our strengths in undercar repair then branching into maintenance services. Brake repair, which was added to the menu in the mid-eighties, now accounts for more than one third of sales. Oil changes, tune-ups and tires were added more recently. And, taking advantage of our expertise in exhaust and the increased popularity of high performance upgrades to small cars and light trucks, we have begun to emphasize performance exhaust installation. All of these additions are designed to encourage consumers to come in on a regular, proactive basis, moving this business from a transaction-driven grudge purchase to the development of a loyal relationship between consumer and service facility.

As the market changed and services were added to Meineke's menu, we began to feel that our name no longer accurately reflected our business reality. Yes, nine out of ten consumers could identify the Meineke name, but if you asked a hundred people what Meineke did, nearly all would say mufflers. Through extensive research, we came to believe that a redefinition of our brand would be critical to our reaching a broad consumer base with our wider range of services. So, in March 2003, we officially changed our name from Meineke Discount Mufflers to Meineke Car Care Center. Consumer perception is extremely important. We feel strongly that our new name is a much better reflection of how the Meineke service facility has evolved and offers huge opportunities to build a broad, loyal customer base.

Advertising has been our second focal point for reaching the consumer. With a relatively small pool of advertising funds, Meineke has consistently looked for ways to reap the largest returns on our advertising investment. The one essential that hasn't changed over the years is our commitment to Yellow Pages advertising. Meineke has consistently been in the top 15 Yellow Pages advertisers in the US and the program is continually reviewed to see that our listings remain competitive in hundreds of primary and secondary directories.

Meineke also relies on a heavy television presence, striving to maximize our total impressions per dollar spent to reach our target audience. We have been fortunate to establish a long-term trusted relationship with our media-buying firm (as well as our Yellow Pages provider). Because of this relationship, we have access to additional research data that helps us better target our message, and to discounts that allow us to spread our advertising dollars that much farther.

Given the generally poor reputation attached to automotive repair facilities by the motoring public, it is no surprise that we believe fostering trust to be the most difficult challenge facing our industry – and a critical element in attracting and retaining customers. Meineke works hard, both before, during and after the purchase, to project an image of trustworthiness.

It starts with our advertising. One of the reasons that we chose George Foreman as the Meineke spokesperson and have retained him for so many years is that consumers rate him high for believability and trust. George lends his friendly, familiar face to the Meineke name and consumers trust that he won't steer them wrong.

Once the consumer enters a Meineke facility, it becomes our task to fulfill the promises that George has made on our behalf. Therefore, our strategy with respect to fixing the customer's car is tied very much to making sure that we convince customers that they can trust us. It can be as simple as taking customers into the service bay and showing them the problem, then repeating the show-and-tell after the repair is completed. Or we will return old parts to the customer on request. In either case, our goal is to assure customers that we have actually done the work we said we would.

One of the biggest hurdles in winning consumers' confidence is overcoming the impression that a repair facility will always try to oversell. What is needed is a tool to help shop staff communicate clearly about needed repairs or maintenance services. Just such a tool was born out of a crisis a few years ago when consumers in California complained that they were being sold products and services, by a major automotive repair chain, that were not needed on their vehicles. A group of leading corporations in the automotive repair industry joined to form the Motorist Assurance Program (MAP). Essentially, MAP developed standards for inspecting vehicles and advising consumers about their condition. Using MAP Guidelines, a technician employs checklists to inspect a vehicle and communicate to the consumer whether a particular part: 1) requires repair to make the car safe to operate, or 2) is simply recommended to be repaired to improve the vehicle's performance, or 3) does not need to be replaced at this time. By employing these standardized communication procedures, Meineke franchisees report that MAP Guidelines have greatly enhanced their ability to raise the level of trust consumers have in their professionalism and ability to do the job.

Customer Service

I do not believe that the basic tenets of customer service have changed in the past twenty years, or in thirty years, or as a matter of fact, maybe ever. Ultimately, customer service is about treating the customer the same way you would like to be treated if you were standing on the other side of that counter: professionally, with dignity and courtesy. As a member of management, it is my job to put systems and training in place to make sure that happens on a regular basis.

In a franchise organization, with independent owner operators in charge of each shop location, standardizing customer interaction presents a considerable challenge. Naturally, training is a primary on-going focus. In addition, we find ways to give our franchisees regular feedback on their customer service performance through surveys, mystery shopping, and reviews of their customer complaint history. I am happy to say that Meineke franchisees take excellent care of their customers. Fewer than

81

two of every 1,000 vehicles serviced by Meineke result in a complaint to the corporate office. However, when a customer is dissatisfied, we want to know about it and have developed systems to make it easy for customers to contact us when necessary (via phone, letter or email). These complaints not only give us the opportunity to retain that customer's business, but also to see that the same problem is not repeated.

Perhaps our best technique for improving customer service has been to take the emphasis off "selling" and put it on "educating" the consumer. Once a consumer becomes a Meineke customer, the obvious task is to take care of that customer's initial problem or request. But equally important, is that we take advantage of the opportunity to educate the customer fully as to the condition of the vehicle and any required or recommended services. In line with our "Car Care Center" philosophy, we are instructing Meineke franchisees that consumers will appreciate being made aware of repair or maintenance needs. These concerns may not necessarily require immediate attention, but might be done at some point in the future. Basically we want to share with the consumer both their needs today and their longer-term issues with respect to the vehicle, without a pressured sales pitch. This approach involves a greater commitment of time given to each customer, time to thoroughly inspect the vehicle and clearly explain the results, and the payoff may not come in additional sales on that day. However, research has shown that when consumers decide to make a repair, they will most often go to the first facility that made them aware of the need. By educating our customers, without applying pressure for an immediate sale, we again reinforce our customers' confidence in our professionalism.

Promoting Success

Given the size and diversity of shops in the Meineke chain, we have a tremendous opportunity to learn from the best practices of our most successful shops in terms of growth, profit and consumer satisfaction – and we share their success stories, strategies, and approaches with other franchisees. While there is often friendly competition among franchisees to excel, we all understand the truth of the cliché that the chain can be no stronger than its weakest link. Consequently, franchisees will go out of their way to support and encourage each other to greater success.

To promote success in the chain globally, Meineke's corporate staff works closely with an elected dealer council. These franchisee leaders meet regularly with management to consult on the direction of the chain, critique corporate initiatives, review advertising campaigns, and strengthen lines of communication. Each council member represents a group of about ten shops and sits on a Regional Council, which meets twice annually. Chairpersons from each of the nine Regional Councils in the US and Canada comprise the National Dealer Advisory Council. Dealer representatives to the councils see to it that local concerns are not overlooked and, at the same time, are able to communicate back to individual dealers a more broad-based perspective of chain-wide policy decisions.

Our Leadership & Coaching Program, which is unique in the franchise industry to my knowledge, offers small groups of franchisees to work together and learn from each other to improve specific shop performance goals. Volunteer teams, of six or seven shops each, band together for a three-month period to compete against other teams to create growth in such measurable areas as Average Repair Order, Jobs Per Ticket, Training Hours Completed and Same Store Sales Growth. Through a process of mentoring, sharing best practices and peer encouragement, franchisees find themselves motivated to take a fresh look at old business strategies. Response to the program from franchisees has been remarkable. So remarkable that what began as a one-time trial has become an on-going program, with a new group of Leadership teams being formed every three months. And the effects of the program long outlast the three-month run. Performance of Leadership shops in the measured performance indicators continues to outpace that of the chain average for months after each program has ended. An added benefit to the Leadership Program is that the corporate management learns as well. Some of the best ideas emerging from this process come from the franchisees themselves and can then be adopted by Meineke and implemented across the chain.

The saying goes that knowledge is power. At Meineke, we believe that information is the key to success at the individual shop level. That's why we have found a number of ways to provide data to franchisees that will allow them to compare their individual shops' performance against that of other shops in their region or in the chain as a whole. On Meineke's dealer-only accessible Intranet, we post considerable data on each shop's sales, with comparable chain numbers. (Franchisees may access specific shop data only on their shops, so their confidentiality is protected.) The site also advises franchisees of exactly which stores are growing the fastest in their area. On an annual basis, Meineke produces a *Report to Franchisees,* which again provides a multitude of specific shop data, both current and historical, along with comparisons to the performance of other shops in the regions and in the chain, and against shops of a similar size. This comprehensive report is, again, one-of-a-kind in the franchise industry and has come to be a staple tool for communicating with Meineke franchisees.

Another way we promote the success of each Meineke franchise through better information is through research. With respect to a franchise's location, we buy market data that tells us about the local market: the number of households, the cars that are in those households, the age of the cars, etc. We then forecast what total amount of automotive services will be sold within a two- and three-mile radius of each shop. This forecast is done on every location on a regular basis then measured against the franchisees' total sales numbers, so we know what market share that each facility has captured. Helping franchisees know how well they've penetrated their market versus how their peers performed is an important benchmark for success.

At the corporate level, we promote success by establishing bonus plans based on either sales or profits. Basically the incentives are based on a combination of company performance and individual performance. Each corporate employee has a bonus plan, half of which is tied to employee specific performance objectives and half tied to the overall profitability of the chain.

Of course, there are no guarantees for success in any business. The best one can do is develop strategies that maximize the potential for success and minimize risk of failure. It is my understanding that every year in America about sixteen percent of all small business fails. Although the Meineke corporation is not a small business, each of our franchisees is a small-business owner. Candidly, franchising, as a whole, is statistically much more successful than independent small businesses. Within the Meineke chain, we lose about four percent of our shops each year, close to the average number for a franchise chain.

Measuring Success

My background is in accounting and I believe strongly that performance goals must be measurable if they are to have any meaning to the business. Meineke sets very specific goals for both the company-owned and the franchised stores. If the store is in a very mature market, we might expect a three or four percent sales growth. If the store is in a new market, and/or it is early in the store's life, then the goal would be much higher.

But a store's total sales cannot be the only benchmark for success. Consequently, we set goals that will help each store achieve those base elements that specifically drive sales. We consider the number of vehicles that come in for service: How many repeat and referral customers? What is the shop's rate of retention of customers who phone before coming in? What percentage of customers gets an estimate but don't authorize the repair? And we also measure what happens to that vehicle once it is in the shop: What percentage is fully inspected? What percentage is sold more than one job (a muffler *and* an oil change, for example)? What is the average repair order (which can be influenced by both pricing and jobs per ticket)?

Clearly, aside from individual store success, the predominant corporate goal is whether or not we achieved our bottom line target. However, just as with the stores, we know the bottom line success for our corporation is driven by a large number of key performance indicators (KPI) and we measure and incentivize someone on every one of these KPI's. Additionally, we continually monitor our market share, and how are we performing in relation to our primary competitors.

Franchise Management

On the front line, monitoring the performance of every shop in the chain is our team of Operations Managers. Each Operations Manager oversees, on average, forty Meineke shops, grouped by geographic territories. Drawing on their broad knowledge base, Operations Managers provide advice and support to franchisees on a variety of operational issues from adding new services to recruiting trade accounts, from running the in-shop point-of-sale computer system to reducing their cost-of-goods. On any given day, an Operations Manager will be teacher, technician, counselor, accountant, corporate spokesperson and friend.

From the day a new shop opens, Operations Managers are instrumental in guiding the shop's success. One of their most powerful tools is an individualized store business plan, drawn up by each franchise owner every year with the help of the Operations Manager. That business plan may include new sales goals, plans to add new service, ideas for improvements to the facility or local advertising strategies. After assisting the franchisee in building a business plan, the Operations Manager returns to the shop periodically to make certain that the franchisee is working at implementing the plan.

In a sense, Operations Manager is a misnomer. They do not manage shops or franchisees. They are, in fact, conduits for information, tutors and – quite often – cheerleaders. It has been our experience that franchisees will do what is in their own economic best interests, and that their best interests generally coincide with the best interests of the chain. Our responsibility is to see to it that the franchisees have the best information, tools and programs at their disposal to make themselves successful.

Franchising is a great way for a corporation to go to market. It is a distribution concept, no more, no less. However, seeing franchisees succeed who have put their heart, soul, and life savings into a business gives me a great deal of pleasure. I consider Sam Meineke, who started this business, to be a mentor. His goal was very simple: he wanted to make his franchisees millionaires. As the CEO of a franchisor, I do not think one could have a better goal than helping your franchisees make themselves successful – and making the corporation successful in the bargain.

Collaborative Management

The vision of Meineke is not just my own. It comes from the collective wisdom of the entire executive team. During wide ranging discussions at an annual senior management retreat, we develop general concepts for the chain, both short- and long-term. Those concepts are then fleshed out in day-long sessions with senior and department level managers, each contributing his or her views about the appropriate direction for the chain to take and strategies to get us there. Strategies are prioritized and assigned to specific departments for implementation.

By the start of each fiscal year, the goals and strategies have been captured in annual business plans for each department in consultation with the vice president directly responsible for that area. The vice presidents have both a financial budget for implementing the plans, as well as a follow-up system that monitors on a regular basis ten to fifteen key issues each month. The various department heads report back to the full management team monthly on the goals and targets set as a result of the group's direction. While departments shoulder individual responsibilities, the success of the plan as a whole is the responsibility of the entire team. Cooperation and collaboration rather than competition are key to successful implementation.

An Emphasis on Training

I am emphatic about the value of training. You simply cannot do too much. Before someone becomes a franchisee, every new owner must complete an intense four-week training program in our corporate headquarters. The course, which runs six 10-hour days per week, covers business management as well as the technical aspects of operating a Meineke franchise. This training delivers the basic set of tools franchisees need to be successful. Through on-going training, franchisees can add more and more tools to their collection.

Operations Managers carry with them thirty-one self-contained training courses to provide to franchisees based upon the needs of each store. Vendors offer training in specific technical applications to local shop groups. In addition, Meineke sponsors annual dealer conventions, which combine extensive educational opportunities with time for networking and relaxation.

Despite our best efforts, delivery of effective standardized training can be difficult to achieve in a franchise chain with stores dispersed across a continent. Besides the geographic challenges, as with most retail businesses, Meineke shops run 60-hour weeks, leaving little time for scheduled training. Short of closing down a store, group staff training must be conducted late in the evenings or on Sundays – not optimal training times. I believe we have found the key to solving this universal problem. As part of our dealer-access Intranet, we established Meineke University On-Line, a series of fifty-three (to date) short, interactive web-based courses available to franchisees, shop managers, technicians and corporate staff any time anywhere. We are the second franchise company (after MailBoxes, Etc.) that I am aware of with such a program. As a course is completed, the trainee takes a short, multiple-choice test and adds the results to his/her course transcript.

Significantly, we can measure separately the sales performance of stores whose staff takes the Internet-based training and those who do not. We have documented a significant difference in their sales performance immediately after they take the courses. For example, prior to each Meineke national sales promotion, we make available a free course with tips on making the most of the sale. And, of course, we find that those franchisees that actually take the course before the sale will outperform those that did not take the course.

If we do a good job of training the franchisees as to the best way to operate their business, then the franchisees will be more likely to find and hire the right kind of people to fulfill those expectations. Candidly, hiring good quality people and keeping them well-trained is the hardest part of our franchisees' job and will continue to be. The training programs Meineke has put into place are specifically designed to improve employee quality. Meineke hires from the same pool of applicants as all our competitors. Our task is to help franchisees identify and hire the best applicants available, then provide the training tools that will add to their skill set and make them real assets to the business.

Changes in the Business

From my point of view, a company's ability to manage change is dependent largely on the quality of its training. For example, in 1996, when I became president of this company, exhaust was 60 percent of our business. There were fifty million units of exhaust sold in the United States in 1996. However, as I mentioned previously, stainless steel arrived and changed all that. As a result, the market for exhaust went from fifty million units in 1996 down to probably eighteen or nineteen million units this year. In fact, 60 percent of the market for exhaust has gone away since 1996.

In spite of this, Meineke has had same-store sales increase virtually every year. We maintained this sales growth through a timely shift in product mix, then supporting those new services through training. Once we understood the trend and its likely impact on the exhaust business, we advised our franchisees that they couldn't make a living in the future if they didn't adapt to the changing times. We thoroughly researched the profitability of a variety of alternate services, recommended the best of those to our franchisees, and eventually changed our name to reflect our broader range of services. In addition to providing information, we've supported these added services by negotiating preferred vendor rates for parts and equipment, run special promotions for new services and highlighted new services in our training programs.

Our business has also been affected by the fact that vehicles are becoming more and more complicated. When something goes wrong, it is not like the old days when you could open the hood and see the problems from the outside. Vehicles now have computer modules that not only tell you when something is broken; they also warn you when something is *about* to go wrong. The computer module may even diagnose the problem and – in some advanced models – make an appointment for you at the nearest repair facility.

A key challenge for us is to make certain that we have the capability of reading those computer codes, which have been installed by the manufacturer, so that we can repair the vehicle. Naturally, auto manufacturers would prefer to keep this data to themselves and force consumers to have repairs made only through the dealerships. We believe this monopoly would be unfair to consumers, severely limiting their repair options, as well as to small repair facilities. In the interest of forestalling such a move, we are talking with members of Congress, our senators and congressmen, specifically on "Right to Repair" legislation. This legislation is essential to enable us to readily obtain from the manufacturer what a car's scan codes are and how to repair them.

Once upon a time, I had a great boss who talked to me a lot about how businesses seem to succeed when they are little, but when they get big, they seem to lose their way. From my perspective the important ingredient that small retailers have and big retailers lack is the touch in communications. When there is one store with one person running it, the owner sees and hears everything. Then as soon as there is a problem, the owner can communicate with the employee directly as to what that problem is and how to correct it. As a result, the employee receives immediate feedback. In order for a large company to be successful, it needs to replicate this small business interaction. Systems must be in place so that the corporation communicates with and trains everyone – not just management or key personnel, but everyone in the organization – regularly. If a business can figure out how to do this better than anybody else, it will ultimately succeed.

Ken Walker, a graduate of the University of Texas, has a wealth of experience, which was gained from over 25 years of service in the automotive aftermarket. Mr. Walker joined Meineke in 1996 after serving 3-1/2 years as President and CEO of Parts, Inc., in Memphis, Tennessee. PI was a distributor of automotive parts and supplies with distribution facilities and stores covering 24 states. Prior to his position with Parts, he spent 17 years in similar businesses, serving as President and CEO of Cardis Corporation from 1989-1992. He previously held positions at AI Automotive (1983 - 1988), and Big 4 Automotive (1976 - 1983). Before entering the automotive aftermarket, he was a manager and CPA with Arthur Young and Company in Fort Worth, Texas from 1970 - 1976.

Mr. Walker is currently a member of the World President's Organization and completed his term as Chairman of the Automotive Warehouse Distributors Association (AWDA) in 1996. He has also served as an instructor for many AWDA Seminars. He is a recipient of the AWDA Memorial Scholarship and Pursuit of Excellence Award. He currently serves on the Education Committee for the Automotive Aftermarket Industry Association (AAIA) and was recently appointed to the International Franchise Association (IFA) Board. Under Walker's leadership, Meineke became the first automotive service chain to earn the American Association of Franchisees & Dealers' prestigious Fair Franchising Seal. In recognition of its exemplary franchisee relations, Meineke was named AAFD's Franchisor of Year in 2001.

Attracting the Customer

Marc C. van Gelder
Peapod
President & CEO

Online Retail

Peapod is America's largest online home delivery grocer service. We deliver basic consumables to our customers on a today-for-tomorrow schedule. If customers order with us today, they can receive delivery as soon as tomorrow. If you look at our company, we are the grand daddy of the online grocers. We started our business in 1989, and we have grown every year. In the year 2000, we changed our strategy to co-branding with supermarkets that are owned by the same parent company (Peapod by Stop & Shop and Peapod by Giant). We leverage the infrastructure and buying power of the stores but do all of our business online. Our business is about convenience – we cater to the busy individual and busy family. We are for the middle-class, mainstream America that wants the convenience of ordering online. That is one piece of the equation. The other piece is that our customers get their groceries home delivered.

Key Differences between Online Retail and Traditional Retail

There are a couple of differences between our online business and traditional retail. First, of course, we do not have physical stores. In the offline world, location is very important. That is less important for us. Rather, the Web site is very important for us. If you look at the offline world versus the online world, one big difference in the online world is the first time you shop with us you are creating a list. Then going forward you can access a list of items you have purchased, this helps speed up the process each time you shop. People in the offline world shop much more impulsively, so if you look at our Web site, we have tried to become more impulse oriented. We try to stimulate impulse shopping through the use of online coupons and suggested items that compliment what you have already purchased.

Physical location and impulse shopping are two of the differences between online and retail stores. The other big difference is that we are really a combination of a supermarket retailer and a delivery company, such as Fed Ex or UPS. We are very much focused on the delivery side of the business, which also provides convenience. We try to optimize the delivery schedule and meet the lifestyle demands of our customers.

Greatest Challenges

Our business is changing. We are growing about 25 percent per year, and we see that growth continuing. There are a couple of external forces that are helping to generate that growth, such as Broadband. Also, more women than men are shopping online, which is helping our business. There are still three major hurdles we need to overcome: One is to get people to try us. They prefer to pick their own tomatoes. Our challenge is to explain that we have "one touch produce." It comes from a farm into a distribution center and goes directly out to the customer.

The second hurdle is that to get people to order from us on a regular basis, we need to get them into the habit of it. Often people begin to develop habits, for instance when the weather is bad, however when it gets nicer, they do not mind going to the store. To get people in the regular habit of ordering every week, that is challenging. The third hurdle is the execution, which really has to do with making the web site fast and easy to navigate, maintaining in-stock items at all times and delivering on time.

Attracting & Retaining Customers – The Approach

One tactic we use in order to get people to try our service is to advertise within the stores of our partners (Stop & Shop and Giant). We do a lot of explaining regarding how we handle our produce, the quality of our products and where we get our goods from. We use billboards, radio and direct mail to get people's attention. We also work with search engine companies to ensure when consumers are surfing the web and type in online groceries, we are the first name that comes up. Once we have attracted a customer, we continue the conversation through email, direct mail and informational flyers with their orders.

We make sure our product selection is a subset of the stores and that we are providing a good assortment of local products. We have about 10,000 items while on average, a grocery store has about 40,000. We select those items by looking at which products best relate to our target market. We also look at which products are fast movers for the stores; determining which sizes and brands the consumers purchase in a traditional retailer helps us round out our mix and provide the best assortment to our customers.

People often shop from their previously created list. If we introduce a new product, we try to get that added to their list. To do this we will include the product in an area of our web site called "New Products/New Introductions." The customer may also see the item within their personal shopping list. In order to enhance the shopping experience, we include the top four sale items within the customer's personal shopping list, so when we have a new item we will feature it on sale. This insures our customers will see the new item. We also include a "new" burst on the item to let customers know it is new to our mix.

We also integrated the loyalty cards from the stores. There is a notion that our site and other grocery sites are not developed as much as Amazon because our customers still shop from the lists, but we do promotions for customers. That is the beauty of the Web. You can do a lot of data gathering and data analysis. We do click-stream analysis of how people buy. We put a lot of effort on growing the basket size, the order size. Three years ago, our average order was $106. Today, it is $143. The way we did that was to look at a lot of cross sells and impulse sells. If you buy peanut butter, we also promote jelly and bread, for example. We looked at making the Web merchandise friendly. You see pictures and you can get nutritional information. You can also sort the information on fat content, calories, and sugar content.

Providing Good Customer Service

Providing good customer service is extremely important. Speed of delivery is very important to customers. In every business, things go wrong. We have a central customer service center in Chicago for the whole country. We try to hire very customer-oriented associates in our call center. We try to solve issues for the customers in a very speedy and customer friendly way. My strong belief is that people tolerate you when you make mistakes but it is how you solve the problem for the customer is what is extremely important. If you solve the problem in a correct way, I think the customers are tolerant and very happy in the end. We keep customer records, and track every interaction a customer has with us, and we can look up the record if necessary.

We also do a lot of customer research. Customers love to give their opinion. Our response rate on the Web is much higher generally than what you get offline. We have a couple of instruments for that. We have the traditional customer research around a certain issue, and we have a service on the Web. We do tracking studies, which are very detailed, where we go back over time to customer groups and ask them about the quality of the service. We go from what their experience with price was to their experience with the product and drivers. The last thing we do is use focus groups, where we invite a group of customers to share their experiences with us and allow them to also share their ideas with us.

Evaluating Risk

A risk we often take is trying new ways to build awareness for the service. We generally start with a smaller test monitoring the effect on our business before we expand on a larger scale. We take risks with products by evaluating our business and adding new products to determine what our payback will be. For instance, if we get a new line of products, we need to look at the potential for the product. That is how we mitigate our risk. Our risk is always based on how the customer is affected. That's the bottom line.

In another respect, when we evaluate a market, the first thing we do is look at busy families with kids, busy professionals, and small business potential. The second area is density, which is important. We do better in more urban areas than rural areas. The first indication of success in a market is how quickly we get new customers in. The second indication is whether the customers are ordering the right order size. The order size is important. You can get customers but if they all write small orders, we do not make any money. The other criterion is transportation, to ensure that our drivers do not get clogged up in traffic.

Visions for the Company

Our vision consists of three things. One is to grow a customer-focused profitable business. The word growth is very important and profitability is very important. The second piece is to motivate our associates. The third piece is to be innovative. We need to be innovative with new products for customers with new technologies and new services. Those are the three goals.

For motivating associates, communication is extremely important. We try to have a very open communication style. The kind of people we attract in the corporate and marketing and merchandising departments are innovative people. We look for people with a passion for the customer and also a passion to innovate. We communicate a lot and we also set people up with individual goals, for which they get incentives.

We retain our associates by motivating them. By motivating people, they feel a part of the team. The company was actually founded by two brothers (Andrew and Thomas Parkinson). They are still with the company. They are still a very important part of the business. They want to make the company succeed. I believe that demonstrates the culture here. People want to stay, to work hard, and we have certain measures in place to encourage them to do so.

Constituting Success

Success is growing profitably. Retaining our key associates and being able to attract new associates is also part of success. We continue to lead the innovation in online grocer retailing, which is another success factor.

Like Stop & Shop and Giant, our growth is going to be on the East Coast. Today, we are in five markets. We are in Chicago, where we started, and we are in Boston, New York-Long Island, New York-Westchester, and Connecticut. We also have a location in Washington DC. There is a lot of opportunity still on the East Coast for us. For example, we are not everywhere in Connecticut yet. We are not in all of Rhode Island. So, we definitely have East Coast focus growth.

Changes in Retail

We see people online with us who may shop at the store another day. There is a blurring of the lines. For your grocery shopping, you do not go to one channel alone. That is one of the biggest changes in retail. The other big change is that people have become very convenience-oriented, which helps us with the growth of our business. Consumers have also become more demanding. They do not go to one outlet for everything, they cherry pick. There are also different moments in people's life and time when they go to different places to shop.

Looking at broad trends, online grocery shopping is still growing at a very healthy rate. Broadband is still continuing to grow, and the Internet is becoming much more mainstream. Your computer is going to become part of your kitchen. That is important for our business.

The grocery business it is not a luxury. People need to eat. We need to deliver good quality groceries in a very efficient manner to survive in these economic times. We try to win the trust of our customers with efficiency and very good quality products.

In our business, everything is less than ten years old. People like change and thrive on change in our company. They see it as a challenge and embrace it. That is a very important component of our business. In retail, you know right away if you are wrong. It is very short-term gratification. If you do something right, you get customer approval right away.

Continued Success

Staying focused with customer needs is one way to maintain success in retail. The second way is to increase order size, and the third would be to have the right associates and train them to be customer focused. I believe challenge, customer focus, and building something new are the components of why people stay in retail and are fulfilled.

Marc C. van Gelder (42) serves as President and Chief Executive Officer of Peapod. Prior to joining Peapod in 2000, Mr. van Gelder held the positions of Senior Vice President, Logistics and Supply Chain Management of The Stop & Shop Supermarket Company from November 1998 through April 2000. Prior to joining Stop & Shop, a wholly-owned subsidiary of Ahold in The Netherlands, Mr. van Gelder held the position of Program Director, Business Development for Ahold from 1996 through November 1998 in the Netherlands, and prior to that, Senior Manager for McKinsey & Company from 1990 through 1996. He received a master's degree in Economics from Erasmus University in Rotterdam, The Netherlands, and an MBA from the Wharton School of Business at the University of Pennsylvania.

The Art of Customer Service

Jeffrey Stone

Tweeter Home Entertainment Group, Inc.
President & CEO

Retail – A Simple Vision

Retail companies get created for a reason. Generally speaking, a customer is looking for a particular product and/or service and a visionary thinks that he can provide this product or service in a better way than currently exists. Or perhaps he feels that there is a unique way to bring a new product category or service to the consumer. In any scenario, the retail exchange involves the transfer of merchandise or services to a paying customer. A customer is someone who blesses the retailer by crossing the store's threshold with a checkbook at the ready. All we have to do, get ready for this – is serve them!

Customer Service as an Art Form

Most retailers have simply forgotten the art of customer service. Someone who enters a store with a need and leaves with a need fulfilled *and* a smile on his or her face is the ultimate definition of customer service.

Customers enjoy shopping for many reasons but one of them is because we are social animals; we like to be among other people. As a result, people are desirous of having a decent experience when they shop. That is what our company, Tweeter, tries to provide. It's amazing how powerful plain, "old fashioned" customer service can be in a new technology world. Tweeter Home Entertainment Group is in the business of selling retail consumer electronics. We sell home audio, televisions, and car stereos to an end user, a customer. Our target audience is a more affluent, more quality conscious and more service-oriented consumer.

Since the company's inception, Tweeter has placed a strong emphasis on the customer. We're not talking bells and whistles here. Just everyday pleasantries like, "What brings you in today?" Or, "If you have any questions whatsoever when you get home, please give me a call." Or even something as simple as a warm smile that makes the customer feel that they are wanted in the store, that the store appreciates their presence along with their patronage. Or one of my favorites in today's automated world, when someone actually answers the phone when you call the store instead of getting lost in phone mail hell.

In stores across America today, it is very difficult to walk into a retail establishment and get a decent shopping experience. Positive human interaction or for that matter, getting anybody to talk to you, the paying customer, is even more rare. On the occasion that you do get greeted or noticed by a store clerk, often their approach or attitude toward you is filled with such disdain that you do not even want to be in the store anymore, let alone purchase anything.

When it actually comes down to it, there is really nothing "visionary" about a retailer's quest to provide an all-too-rare, positive customer service experience. It just seems that somewhere in the evolution of retailing, friendly service provided by real live human beings was uprooted and replaced by...nothing.

The Retailer as a Consumer

We are all consumers. This is a fact that many retailers seem to ignore, otherwise, they would be treating customers as they would like to be treated themselves. In my opinion and from countless conversations with consumers as a group, retailers barely achieve the lowest level of a consumer's expectations.

At a recent all-company meeting which took place in major cities across the country over a two-week period, 3500 Tweeter associates were asked to raise their hand if they had been the recipient of a great or positively memorable shopping experience during the last year. Only about twenty people raised their hand. Only twenty people in a group of 3500 in nine major cities in America! When asked, "How many of you have had a miserable or totally bland and forgettable experience in a retail establishment during the last year" it seemed as if every hand in the place was in the air!

Competition has increased across America in every facet of retailing and as a result, management teams have been forced to reduce expenses and often people are the first to go. What retailers may forget is that they are spending billions of dollars in advertising driving customers into their establishments. Why spend money to drive customers to your store if you are not prepared to serve them? It doesn't make sense.

Never underestimate the value of a genuine relationship with your customer. If you provide real service, if you honestly *care* about the customer and the reasons that they are in your stores, the customer can tell. Not only does the customer know that you care, but he or she will reward you by coming back time and time again to make purchases. And, they will tell their friends about the service that they received, just as you would tell yours if you were in their position. All this, simply because you treated them with the attention and respect that they *thought* that they were going to get in your store in the first place.

Keeping Your Customers

At Tweeter, we have a very high repeat shopping rate with our customer base. We have a sales staff that not only has the ability but also the desire to answer questions when customers come into the stores. And, who are trained to identify what the customer's needs are and make them happy.

But, it doesn't stop there for Tweeter, and it shouldn't for other retailers either. Keeping your customers means making a personal or professional connection with them. Follow up is key. When was the last time that you received a personal call from a salesperson to ask if you were satisfied with the product that you just bought?

Tweeter customers know that if they have any problems or questions with the product once they get it home, they *own* the salesperson. They own the salesperson because in our company the sales team understands the value of a satisfied customer and what it means to his or her future financial success, as well as the success of the company. Our sales staff will actually go to a customer's house, if need be, to make sure that the customer is satisfied with their purchase, if they are having difficulty setting it up or trouble making it work. Customer service does not end when the customer leaves the store after making a purchase. It's an ongoing relationship. This ongoing relationship adds value to the customer's piece of mind. There is a huge difference between saying or marketing that you do things like this and *actually* doing it. The customer knows the difference because they are much smarter than they used to be!

Personal Perspective on Values and Management

Culture creates the company, not the other way around. Our goals for our company are pretty straightforward. As individuals and as a group we MUST be committed to being the absolute best that we can be in all facets of how we "do" our business. We want the customer experience to be "World Class." We want the company to be viewed by all of the associates who work at Tweeter as a "best in class employer." We want the brand name "Tweeter" to be perceived by the public as one of the leading retail brands, and in effect, stores of all time. We are driven to these goals.

To understand the management style and culture that I try to promote at Tweeter, I feel that it would be best to give you some insight into my life. I believe in God. I believe that God put us on earth for whatever his reasons are and that we are here for a very finite period.

Given that we are here for such a very short time, don't we as individuals and as a group want to have a positive impact in some way? I was not blessed with the intelligence to be a doctor so I cannot save lives nor do I have the gift of science to be able to cure diseases. But, I can and want to lead a group of committed people to excel in whatever it is that we are doing.

Giving a half-hearted effort only produces, if you're lucky, half-effective results and it is also a waste of the limited time we have to make a positive contribution in the world. Are you going to go to work today and give it all you have or are you going to "mail it in"? When you come right down to it, it's just a matter of attitude. I have tried to get this point across repeatedly to my team over the years and it is one of the truths that drive me.

I was raised by parents who held very high moral ethics and values and my dad had a superhuman work ethic. Proudly, I am as my parents were. I believe that my values and ethics have attracted people to the company – not just fellow workers but investors and business partners. And I suppose that others who could not identify with who I am have chosen not to work for or become involved with the company.

One of the things that we share as an organization, and discuss frequently is that there is a group of people at Tweeter who share the same ethics, the same morals and the same goals. We share a passion and a desire for trying to be successful, for wanting to be the best and for treating people that we work with respectfully. That is culture. I do it, the guy in the next office over does it, the woman down the hall does it, the manager in

Boston does it and the salesperson in San Diego does it. There becomes a consistency of spirit in who we are as people, how we act as people, how we perform as a group, how we treat our customers and business partners. That is culture.

My management style is collaborative. Though I am not afraid to make decisions nor do I shy away from that responsibility, I do believe in a participative management approach. Twenty heads think better than one.

One or two times a year the senior management team goes off-site to brainstorm. Leaving the "four walls" of the corporate office and dedicating time for heated debates on industry topics or strategic direction has been a method that we have employed to steer the ship for the last ten years. These off-site summits have helped us to fine-tune direction, agree on important business decisions and have enabled us to return to the office with clear heads to execute our plans. It also helps build upon the general camaraderie of the group and aids in the furthering of the company's culture.

As a boss, I think that I am fairly benevolent but I definitely have an edge that stems from my desire to run a successful enterprise. Like most company leaders, I want to push others to be as successful as they can be.

When people agree with the values that a company's leadership creates, they will stay around for a long time and you end up building a great culture and hopefully, a successful team and business.

Finding the Right People

As we have grown, the importance of having the right people in the right places has become abundantly clear. At Tweeter, our turnover rate at the executive or middle management level is very low. We also have very little turnover at the store manager level. If people do not like what you, as executive management, do, they vote with their feet.

Finding people who share our company's values is as important to Tweeter as finding people who have a passion for what they do. There are so many businesses across the country where there is no passion, no excitement in the workforce.

We look for people who have some zing to their personality. They don't necessarily have to be audio/video enthusiasts but they have to have a passion about something. We look for people who are honest, hardworking, and respectful. Our training program can take just about anybody who has a desire and turn him or her into a stellar salesperson. If you find people who have passion within them, you can get them excited about almost anything. When you go into a store or restaurant and someone greets you with passion and enthusiasm, you are much more likely to buy.

We want people who care. Care about what? It doesn't matter, just as long as they have the gene that makes them care. For some reason, there are many people working in the marketplace that just don't care about you or me or much else for that matter. People who care *want* to provide a good experience for the customer. People who care are conscientious – and people who are conscientious rarely let a company, co-worker or customer down!

Simply put, in my opinion the greatest products, services and strategies come in a distant second, third and fourth place to having the best people to execute the business plan.

Elements of Location

Location is incredibly important to a retail business. Areas where there is heavy retail traffic are the most desirable. As a mid-size specialty retailer new to many geographic areas, many times we do not have the national brand recognition, market share or advertising clout that allows us to stand alone in a marketplace.

We look for areas that naturally hold a high customer traffic level, such as regional malls or power strip centers with an abundance of retail activity. We also like to be near our larger competitors, within a half-mile if possible, because often when customers are spending a significant amount of money, they will comparison shop with competitors who are in close proximity.

In some ways, our competitors' advertising helps drive customer traffic into our stores. We certainly spend a fair amount of money on marketing ourselves, but we find that by being in the right locations where there is steady retail traffic, people will see our sign and come in and check us out.

Most Challenging Aspects of Retail

In my opinion, the business of managing change will be one of the key attributes of a successful retailer in the future. The "change pace" has accelerated. It is not something that happens occasionally; rather it is literally part of everyday business life. This reality means that the organization must be geared for change, embrace change and be on the look out to constantly create change.

So many elements of running a retail company are in real time evolution. The marketplace seems to change daily due to evolving population shifts both in age and ethnicity, as well as constant product changes, technology changes (faster than we can adapt) and competitor changes. Management teams need to be aware of these morphing dynamics in order to keep the company directed. It is your job as a retailer to monitor these changes and adapt to best serve your customer.

The competitive landscape over the last ten years has evolved dramatically. Not just in consumer electronics, but in the retail business in general. Someone different seems to be entering or exiting our categories every month. In every city there seems to be more and more stores competing for the same discretionary dollar. Ten years ago there were just a couple of retailers in every marketplace. Now you have Tweeter, Best Buy, Circuit City, Wal-Mart, Target, and many other retailers in every market along with smaller regional retailers. Seven or eight years ago there were just little regional bookstores. Now there are ten or fifteen Barnes & Noble and Borders in every major market competing with the smaller stores.

Maintaining a talented retail store sales team is also a challenge. Earlier, I touched upon turnover on a management level, but now let's view salesperson retention. Typically retailers have triple digit turnover, yes – over 100 percent in any given year. On average we have run between 16 and 35 percent turnover in our sales organization, which is much lower than most other companies.

Maintaining a seasoned sales team is a challenge when the economy is good just as it is a challenge when the economy is bad. Night and weekend work is required and that sometimes creates conflicts on the home front, especially for folks with families.

We have a great reputation among our associates for treating them well. I believe that our turnover being much lower than the majority of retailers is illustrative of the fact that we are doing something right in terms of how we treat people and is reflective of our culture in general.

In Tweeter's retailing world, technology can be a challenge as well. The products are becoming more and more technologically confusing. Our goal is not only to understand and explain the technology in the store, but also to be able to take the product to the customer's home and install it.

Our customer just wants to enjoy the lifestyle and benefits that our products help create. We have to possess the skill to install the product in a customer's home so that they merely have to press a button to control all of their electronics. This end-user simplicity in installation is one of the roads that we, as a company are moving down. Our skill with installing and integrating our products is going to be a place that will allow us to thrive and compete very successfully in the future. The products that we sell will still be important but what will become more important are the services that we provide for the customer. A twenty thousand dollar system is great, but if you need six remotes and a teenager to operate it, it's not as enjoyable. It's our job to solve this problem for the customer.

Profits Matter

Our ability to make profits has everything to do with understanding who we are and who we are not, within the marketplace. This is important because it keeps us from spinning our wheels (wasting money) and allows us to stay focused on things that match our strategy and service our customers, therefore adding to the bottom line.

For years, we have educated our management team at every level about the profit and loss statement. Store and department managers and department heads are accountable for their sales, gross margin and area expenses. They are paid bonuses relative to their achievement levels against the operating budget. We are rigorous with monthly reporting so that people see their report cards to understand their progress and productivity. As a for-profit enterprise, our organization understands that the creation of shareholder value is not an option, but a requirement.

It is important that an organization understands that profitability matters and also, what defines profitability. If the organization's bonus and compensation plans are not tied into profitability but directed elsewhere, the organization may in fact achieve all its goals but its members may find themselves in the unemployment line as a result of bankruptcy.

Characteristics of a Profitable Product

Products that really help you define and maintain your image while making a profit are critical to store brand success. Today that product for Tweeter is flat panel TV. The "cool factor" of these products is attracting the customers to the store in droves.

Tweeter's goal is to own the market position as the flat panel experts. Television is moving from big square boxes that take up half of the living room to sleek flat televisions that hang on a wall, enhancing the décor rather than detracting from it. Flat panel TV is all about a lifestyle and a look. Most women, in particular, hate those big TVs that take up their living room. Flat panel technology is the most important change in television since the inception of color TV and Tweeter is in a great position to support the millions of customers who will want to make the switch to a wall-hanging TV in this digital age.

Looking Toward the Future

Smart retailers pay attention to the other major players in their industry. They shop competitors' stores and read their press releases so that they understand what it is they are doing to be successful and different in the marketplace. We believe that this is critical to business success and one's competitive standing.

In order to compete in the future, retailers will need to carve out a niche of specialization in order to be unique, or be the absolute low cost provider, to avoid being just another "me too" retailer. What your unique selling propositions are and how they are valued by your customer base, or potential customer base, will determine your success. Over the years, Tweeter has communicated its unique selling propositions, which are based on quality products that are not available in the mass-market channel, an incredibly knowledgeable sales team and an organization focused on service.

Our challenge over the next three to four years is to evolve our strategy as technology evolves while staying focused on our customers' needs. A successful retailer is aware of how their environment and customers change over time

Measuring Success

From our vantage point, there are three components to determining true retailing success. Some companies have only one or two of the components. We believe that the "Best of the Best" have all three. We need to ask ourselves three questions. "How do our customers view us?" "How do our associates view us?" And finally, "Are we profitable?"

First, does the customer enjoy their experience when they shop with you? This is measured by repeat traffic. If you can capture the customer's name and address on your company's point-of-sale computer, you can determine how frequently they come back to shop. If you repeatedly see an abundance of your customers coming to shop in your stores, you have passed the first measurement of success.

Secondly, and the most obvious indicator of a retailer's success, is profitability. Any company can give away merchandise or drive sales by cutting retail prices but not make any money. Sometimes the customer does not understand this. Being profitable ensures that we can exist to serve them another day.

And finally, as mentioned earlier, a company's associate turnover rate is to a great extent a measure of its success. If turnover is low, it means that the heart and soul of the company is "doing the right thing" for its employees.

Customers, employees and profits – if you can create an environment where the first two love you, the third always follows!

Jeffrey Stone came to Tweeter with years of specialty retail experience that began in the furniture industry. He started his career at Levitz Furniture in Dedham, MA, and in 1984 Mr. Stone moved to Scandinavian Design, a Massachusetts-based upscale furniture chain, where he served first as Human Resources Manager and then Vice President of Human Resources and Training.

Recruited by Bread & Circus, a highly regarded specialty Natural Foods supermarket chain, Mr. Stone became their Vice President of Human Resources/Training in 1987, and was charged with developing a professional management group in a company that had become an emerging enterprise. Later that year he became Executive Vice President, responsible for overseeing the business and a key contributor in the health food chain's rapid growth and success.

In 1990, Tweeter Home Entertainment Group's Board of Directors were looking for a new President and chose Stone to fill the position. Stone took on the role of CEO in January 1999. As President and CEO, Stone has been instrumental in managing the company's enormous growth over the past ten years as the chain has grown from 13 stores in three New England states in 1990 to its present day total of 177 stores in 21 states. He has been responsible, with company founder Sandy Bloomberg, for the company's strategic direction and overseeing the company's successful operations. In 2002, the company reported $796 million in revenue.

A native of Abington, MA, Mr. Stone received his B.A. in Business from Upsala College, New Jersey. Mr. Stone serves as President of his church's congregation, sits on the Board of Advisors for two small companies and is active in three local charitable organizations.

The Principles of Retailing

Kip Tindell
The Container Store
CEO, President and Co-Founder

Selling the Hard Stuff

We created the storage and organization category of retailing in 1978 when we opened our first store in Dallas, Texas in a 1,600 square foot space. Back then, many of the products we wanted to sell were only available for commercial use. The common denominator of all of the products was that they would save you valuable space and time. That was and still is the mission of The Container Store – to offer multifunctional, well-designed storage and organization solutions that will save our customers valuable space and time. We do this while providing the highest level of customer service.

When my partner Garrett Boone and I opened that first store, we had a goal: to create the perfect retail store. We're not quite there yet – we'll probably never be there – but we'll continue to shoot for that goal, constantly reevaluating and improving upon our business. Because we really have no reason to exist if we are doing the same thing that everyone else is doing. The discount stores do far too good a job of selling commodity-type products. They compete on price and convenience; we do something that is somewhat the opposite of that. We take products that are actually very hard to sell and require an exceptionally high service level on the part of our salespeople.

Our core competency is service, and it has to be in order to sell these "hard to sell" types of products, which include things such as component shelving systems and modular drawer systems – fairly complex things that require a great deal of product knowledge and a lot of communication between the customer and the salesperson. The products that we sell the best tend to languish on the shelves of a mass-merchant retailer. They just don't sell themselves, they have to be explained. That affords us an opportunity to differentiate ourselves through our products and service level, and it also somewhat insulates us from competition because very few retailers are willing to invest in the significant resources needed to attract, train and retain highly talented and motivated employees.

In fact, the average retailer invests eight hours of formal training in a first-year, full-time employee. We provide more than 241 hours. This commitment to training, to making sure our employees are armed with the knowledge to help our customers solve their storage problems, helps set us apart as the storage and organization experts. And it has certainly been a huge factor in the success of our company over the past 25 years.

The more dedicated and the more knowledgeable your sales staff is, the higher your sales are. There is a direct relationship between information, training and development on the part of the sales staff and revenues.

Building a Culture

Back when I was a high school student at Jesuit College Prep in Dallas, I started what I called my "philosophy epistle." It was a file where I'd drop various anecdotes, musings and just good old philosophical phrases that I admired – things that I was taught throughout the years, earth-shattering thoughts from professors or philosophers and other things that may have just scrolled through my mind. But I was really selective of what I kept in that file.

During my time at Jesuit, the things in the file were more on a philosophical level and as I started college, they took more of a business slant. I still had this file when Garrett and I started The Container Store. This philosophy epistle really was a reflection of the way I operated – whether it was personal or business related. It had a lot to do with the way we ran the business.

When we opened our Houston store, back in 1988 – ten years later – I pulled some of these thoughts out of that coveted file and we put on paper the six Foundation Principles™ that are at the heart of our business today.

You see, the Houston store made us take a look at our business a little harder. We held out for ten years for that coveted retail space at Post Oak and Westheimer. And we did more business with that store than we'd ever done before, probably five times more than what we had ever experienced. Everyone was overwhelmed. All of the employees just couldn't "get together" and act as a unit and the store wasn't operating as the same company we were in Dallas. We weren't bound together. So I called a meeting with all of the Houston employees. I struggled with how I was going to inspire everyone – I had to figure out some way to draw us together so that the business we were operating in Houston was the same as in Dallas. It was a very critical time in our history.

As I was trying to decide what to say, I dipped into my file – my old Jesuit epistle file – for assistance, because we saw a need to put some business philosophies down on paper. What resulted was our six Foundation Principles™. They would let our employees know that no matter how big we got – these six sort of "do unto others" principles, instead of the typical retail phone book-sized procedural manual, would help guide us, keep us on track, stay focused and keep us all happy as employees. And the success with the bottom line would come naturally.

Finding Great People

We've been very fortunate to have been selected number one on *FORTUNE* magazine's annual list of the "100 Best Companies to Work For in America" in 2000 and 2001 and number two on the 2002 and 2003 lists. One of the key reasons The Container Store is a great place to work is the people we hire.

One of our Foundation Principles™ is that "one great person is equal to three good people," in terms of business productivity. If you really believe that one great is equal to three good, why hire anyone other than a great person? Great people are very hard to find, so it requires not just a recruiting department, but everyone in the company participating in the recruiting efforts. It requires quite a bit of bravery because we actually will approach a person that we think is right for our culture and right for our business. We've been known to recruit people down the aisles of our stores. Our customers make the best employees and most of our employees come from the ranks of our enthusiastic customers. It comes down to a belief in the product and a belief in the culture and a belief in the business.

We pay 50 to 100 percent above industry average. If you really believe that one great is equal to three good, you have to put your money where your mouth is. It takes more bravery to pay great people well, particularly in retail. You can afford to pay someone twice what someone else might, and everyone wins. The company wins because it is getting three times the productivity at only two times the payroll cost, and the employee wins because they are being paid double what someone else might pay them. Most importantly, the customer wins because they are getting uncommonly great customer service from a great employee.

Once we find and hire those great people, we keep them informed with what's going on in the company. I believe that a very important aspect of leadership is making sure that everyone knows where the company is heading and how we're going to get there. We share everything with our employees – daily sales results, expansion plans and more. You might call it over communicating. It breeds a lot of loyalty, a lot of unity, and a lot of teamwork.

123

Service = Selling

We focus a lot on values-driven leadership. Another of our Foundation Principles™ is "fill the other guy's basket to the brim, making money then becomes an easy proposition." It's an old Andrew Carnegie analogy. This is quite the opposite of the old J.R. Ewing way of doing business. It's all about creating a mutually beneficial relationship with the people you do business with, and doing everything you can for them. I truly believe if you want to make a lot of money in a short period of time, this is the best way to do it. People really want to do business with people that they trust and respect.

Once you craft this mutually beneficial relationship, and it takes a lot of work, you end up being the store that everyone raves about and your vendors' favorite customer. We pay our vendors on time – sometimes early – and we do whatever we can to help "fill their baskets." This could mean taking inventory a little early into our Distribution Center, or placing a large order to help cut their costs. These relationships we've developed with our vendors provide an incredibly competitive edge for a company like ours against the big box retailers who have volume buying power.

As for our stores and our employees, we know that when we provide that exceptionally high level of customer service and really "astonish" our customers, they will come back to us again and again. They'll come back when they have other storage challenges, they'll tell their friends about us and they'll truly become customers for life. We like to say that service is equal to selling – they're one in the same.

The Right Products

For the past 25 years, we've remained committed to our concept of storage and organization – no one else has focused solely on storage and organization products like The Container Store. We also like to offer products that the rest of the world does not offer, which helps differentiate us. Of course, the design of a product is very important, but it has to function well first and foremost.

Storage and organization products keep getting better and better. It's a bit like the computer industry or the evolution of the calculator. They used to be big and clunky and slow and expensive, and now they are fast and small and great. That is what is happening in the housewares industry. The products of today are nothing compared to the products of tomorrow. As we grow in size, we're able to work with manufacturers to create better and better products. And as the storage and organization industry evolves, more and more bigger manufacturers are going to risk more capital to develop products that fit this category.

Opening New Stores

Many people involved in human resources and marketing and merchandising would like to think that location is not that important, but it is *terribly* important. If you have the greatest store of its kind around, why hide it? Excellent locations are the right thing for any type of business. You gain from that. Why not get the very best real estate that you possibly can? We will hold out forever for a perfect location. We are constantly looking at all markets and working hard on 25 or 30 different locations, and when that one great location becomes available, that is when we open that location. The difference between an excellent location and a very good location is immense in terms of profitability.

It's very important to have wonderful visibility and demographics. It's also vital to know exactly who your core customer is, who your target customer is. What are their affinities? How densely that location attracts people of that affinity type is crucial.

It's also important to realize that an incremental 10 percent in revenue can have a gigantic increase in a retailer's earnings. We do a very interesting thing with Crate & Barrel. Most retailers are so paranoid of each other that they are afraid of being located next to each other. Many people think that we compete with Crate & Barrel. We get checks written out to Crate & Barrel and they get checks written out to The Container Store. We only have about two percent exact crossover in our product offerings. We are not competitors, but we do attract exactly the same target customer. What we really ought to be doing – and do – is locate ourselves right next door to each other to completely serve the customer wherever we can, creating a one-stop shopping opportunity. That is the exact opposite of what most typical, paranoid retailers do. By locating next door to each other, we get about a 20 percent crossover. When we do that, we also try to attract other retailers to locate next to us that we think have the same target customer.

When we open a new store, we take a slightly different approach than other retailers. We begin developing an advertising, marketing and public relations plan nine to twelve months out. We begin to hire the staff for that new store early – as much as several months ahead of time. We want them to participate in the setup of the store, from putting the fixtures up to putting the final touches on the displays so that it is truly the new staff's store and not the store of people from the home office. We like to move five to eight core, long-term, experienced people from other locations to the new store when we can. Trainers from across the country help train the new staff, and employees from the home office are in the store helping to develop these new employees. This significantly helps to really infuse the company's unique culture into the new store and staff.

When the doors open, we want it to function as a mature store. We really want our customers' first experience with the store to be exciting. We are really shooting for an A+ store from day one. It takes a lot of planning and a lot of marketing effort to open a store this way, but it pays off when that store immediately begins performing like a mature store.

Thriving on Change

We are completely unafraid of change. We constantly try to analyze everything that we are doing, while staying focused and loyal to our core concept of storage and organization. We are still dedicated to exactly the same thing we were in 1978; we are just doing it better and better.

I think we have created a culture that embraces change and is accustomed to continuing to go onward and upward and improving what we are doing. Our unofficial internal mascot is Gumby. You have to be flexible – to be "Gumby" – and to realize that anything can change, and probably will. We can always do anything better. And nothing is just "your job" or "my job." We all feel very responsible for everything, yet we are efficient and effective in reaching our goals.

We never change for change's sake, though. We just change when we innovate in a way that we think we can do something even better. Improvement and change go hand-in-hand. I think there is a lot of trust on the part of the employees as it pertains to change. And because of that trust, there's a lot of loyalty that the company receives from those employees. When we make a big change, people don't necessarily immediately start worrying how it will affect them personally. Their first thought is that they are secure and that this is going to be better than the way that we used to do it.

The State of Retail

Today, there are fewer and fewer specialty stores. There are even fewer and fewer department stores and fewer and fewer discounters. It is a highly competitive environment that demands excellence and innovation, and that is a thrilling environment to be in. I do think that in spite of the shrinking nature of the field, the customer is winning. Retailers are forced to do more for the customer than the competition or they simply won't survive. You have to be truly great at what you do in the U.S. retail industry in order to survive. That is a definite "plus" for the consumer and wonderful for the industry.

I think retail is the greatest medium there is. It involves people; it involves merchandising. At The Container Store, you get to help solve people's problems, bring a little order to their lives, and perhaps a smile to their faces. Our goal is to get people excited about their newly-organized closet, pantry, or drawer. If they are happy, then they will show that closet to their next-door neighbor or sister-in law. When you can generate that emotional response, you get customers who are inviting friends and neighbors into their homes to show off their organized closets – and that kind of endorsement, as we all know as merchants, is priceless!

It's important for retailers to offer product solutions that transcend value. If you have a product that costs 20 percent more than something else, but is 300 percent better looking and functions 500 percent better and lasts 600 percent longer, that is true *value*. We talk about transcending value by finding products that, although they may be hard to sell, solve the customer's problems in such a way that they really evoke that emotional response. Again, it takes wonderful salespeople to help customers understand the value in an item, but once it's explained, it is an easy thing to sell.

It is almost oxymoronic that a *retailer* could be a great place to work. Most people think it would be quite the opposite. We are, in our own modest way, trying to do something about that and trying to help other retailers believe that hiring only *great* people is possible. You can't get great people to work in a retail store unless you really believe it is possible.

We measure success by how profitable we are, but profitability isn't everything. I think more than most businesses, we companion that with a measurement against how well the culture is growing and the Foundation Principles™ are being practiced. You know you are successful when you can sense, feel, and see evidence of participation in the brand by everyone – your customers, vendors and your employees.

Kip Tindell is the CEO, President and Co-Founder of The Container Store. While still in high school, he took a job working in the paint department at Montgomery Ward in 1969. Not only did Tindell become a superstar salesperson, but he also forged a close friendship with Garrett Boone, his future business partner. That friendship lasted through Tindell's college years as an English major at The University of Texas, and at Storehouse, a chain of lifestyle furniture stores, in Austin in 1972. Tindell worked his way through college at Storehouse, where Boone was a regional manager. After college, Mr. Tindell authored a syndicated column on Southwest regional literature, featuring the state's top fiction writers.

At the same time, Mr. Tindell's talent for retailing continued to thrive, and after kicking around the idea of opening a store with Boone for almost 10 years, the two decided to embark on a quest to launch a new retail concept. Initially, almost all of the products that they wanted to sell were developed for commercial use only and were not available to consumers. But once manufacturers realized the prospect of a profitable consumer market for its products, they were eager to supply them. And many of those commercial products defined Boone and Tindell's original concept – to sell multifunctional, storage and organization products that would save customer's space and time.

With the products selected, and an initial investment of $35,000, The Container Store's first location at Preston Road and Forest Lane in North Dallas was unveiled in 1978. The store outgrew its space within a year, and by 1980 had expanded twice. Twenty years later, The Container Store has 28 stores across the country, which average 25,000 square feet. With 2003 sales projected at over $335 million, the originators of the storage and organization category of retailing remain the leaders in an industry that continues to thrive.

Mr. Tindell continues to embody the unique corporate culture he created, which empowers employees to use their own intuition and creativity to solve problems – instead of referring to the proverbial procedural manual. Thus, he has nurtured a fierce loyalty to the company, which has an incredible number of career employees – who might never have dreamed of a career in retail. In fact, that culture has propelled The Container Store to the top of FORTUNE magazine's list of "100 Best Companies To Work For In America" four years in a row.

He is also actively involved in the community as a member of the Salesmanship Club, a non-profit organization dedicated to serving families in the Greater Dallas area, and the Save the Cathedral campaign, a restoration project for Dallas' century-old Cathedral Guadalupe. He will also serve as a 2003 board member for both Goodwill Industries and the National Retail Federation (NRF).

Orvis – Multi-Channel Retailing…

of an Authentic Lifestyle

Perk Perkins

The Orvis Co.
President & CEO

The Brand and The Lifestyle

Our brand, our company and our activities communicate a lifestyle. We provide an atlas to what we call "distinctive country living" and the reinforcements are multifold. It is through the goods we sell, the conservation work we sponsor, the sporting traditions we endorse, and the schools and seminars we run that we communicate this lifestyle. This is reinforced further through the imagery that we place on our web site and in our catalog. We're saying, "This is what that lifestyle looks like."

From a more mechanical standpoint, we distribute our brand message through a number of different channels:
We are the nation's oldest catalog company, through which we do the majority of our sales.
We have a chain of over 30 retail stores.
We have a classic wholesale distribution system, through which we sell at wholesale to other retailers.
We do a sizable e-commerce business.
We offer an extensive program of schools and classes, with lessons around the lifestyle, which we strive to communicate through our brand image. People can learn to fly fish or to shoot a shotgun; individuals can even learn to become a more effective conservationist.

We differentiate ourselves from our competitors with an acute attention to detail and an insistence on authenticity. This is evident in our catalog work. For instance, dogs are a big part of living in the country, so in our dog catalog, we offer the merchandise that dog owners need and we focus on specific breeds. It is through addressing breeds specifically, even incorporating the breeds' history into the catalog, that we can speak directly to customers. There is an opportunity there to connect with customers and to incorporate a level of authenticity. This is somewhat unique to our business and our approach. This aspect is a direct reflection of my family, who owns and operates this business, and our insistence on authenticity.

A brand has a personality, just as a human being does. And as a human being is known by certain characteristics, a brand is known by certain attributes. For our brand, there are 14 core attributes that we refer to as our brand DNA. We are highly conscious of all our brand messengers, constantly asking, "What are the things we do that relay our brand to our customers?" There are many. For example, it can be our logo, our style of service, our products themselves, the ways in which we construct and design displays, the copy we write and the voice through which those written messages are communicated – each are equally important. The teams that are responsible for these channels of communication understand our brand attributes, and they know they're expected to relay these attributes through their particular media. The end result is to communicate consistently from all sides and through various channels of a diversified company.

One of the core attributes, as I've mentioned above, is authenticity. The individuals writing an advertisement, or those creating a sign for a product, must ask themselves "Am I communicating in an authentic way?" This is of critical importance to our brand and to our business. Two other attributes deliver the message that our brand – and everything that stands behind it – is credible and knowledgeable. These three reinforce each other. We're not a hype company and we maintain this grounded honesty by constantly asking ourselves key questions, such as, "Are we using facts and research? What's believable about what we're saying? Are we speaking knowledgably?"

All of these speak to a similar way of communicating the brand. Two other attributes are important to the brand DNA: tradition and respect. We stand for tradition. When communicating with customers, we want to do so in a way that respects both the customer's knowledge of, and the value that they place upon, tradition. We are not going to use hip, current language or describe a product as the latest thing because our brand doesn't stand for the latest thing; it stands for the timeless thing. These are crucial points for everyone on our team to keep in mind – whether they're a copywriter, a graphic designer or a salesperson on the floor. The consistency of the message delivered is essential to the image and ultimately, to the success of the brand.

Controlling the brand message across the many channels through which we operate is a challenge. It's easier through the catalog and the web site, as that content comes from a central ad department where we have time to control and approve everything before it goes to print or is posted on the web site. But in retail stores, as well as with our dealers, it's much more challenging because in those environments your most vocal messengers are the sales associates, so they must really understand and communicate the brand on its core attributes.

The Team Talent - Managing and Empowering Employees

I'd characterize my management style with three key points. First, I have an unflagging dedication to the strategic plan, the big picture. Second, I pay great attention to detail. I believe vehemently that the small details make the difference in achieving excellence. Finally, I insist on individual accountability. I like everyone in the company to know their key performance metric and how they're performing against their metrics on a weekly basis. Everyone is to have two primary or key measures of performance: one from a quality standpoint and the other from a financial standpoint. For me, the two are: brand equity – I want ours to be the greatest brand in America; and return on equity – I want to deliver an above-average return on equity to our shareholders.

As the metrics vary by an individual's role within the company, the hiring process varies as well. With the sales staff, we're big believers in the idea that you hire for attitude and you train for skills. If we want to provide personal and friendly customer service, we need to hire people who are personal and friendly. We train them how to sell. We don't look for someone who has necessarily had a great history in sales, attitude is much more important. At the manager level, we look for someone who can be the role model for personal and friendly service, with both a pleasing demeanor and a solid background in retail. They're bringing their own skills and knowledge. They're out there on their own, without a lot of corporate support on a daily basis, so we need managers who are going to captain their stores with a fair amount of conviction and experience to begin with.

We empower other executives in two ways. One is fairly traditional – they run their business on an individual level. They have a business defined by sales, profit goals, and the approved budget. Their boundaries are delineated by three things: 1) the strategic plan, 2) the financial goals, and 3) our brand DNA. Within those boundaries, the individual is free to run the business as they see fit. The other method of empowerment is to encourage them to buy-in on those three things from the beginning. Otherwise, individuals won't feel their own power. If they feel they're being dictated to, all the empowerment in the world won't matter, because it won't happen. In one-on-one meetings, we talk through these things to encourage them to take ownership from the outset.

Store managers are then evaluated on a financial and a quality basis. The financial evaluation is the bottom line of the store. Based on past experience, we set a bottom-line goal for the year. Evaluations on a quality basis are based on customer service ratings, derived from secret shopper services. They might be pointed toward a certain category that was rated low last year that we want them to work on this year. In general, although they may vary in degree from one location to another, store managers are evaluated with these two metrics in mind.

In terms of retention, it is our culture that keeps people here. We describe it as an environment of integrity and mutual respect that is rich in praise and recognition. Our wages and career opportunities are competitive, which is attractive. But ultimately, we retain our employees through our culture.

Defining and Measuring Success

Several characteristics denote successful products. Part of the determination of our success rests on the mechanical approach of what is known as GMROI - Gross Margin Return On Inventory, a form of return on investment. It's a mathematical calculation, the bottom-line approach. But often, these figures aren't accessible until the season is partly over. The other indicator of a successful product is one that generates staff enthusiasm, which often results from the training and the display approach taken to position the product. Thirdly, a product's success is determined by the degree to which there is a clear reason for purchasing it. If one product is great, three versions of it aren't necessarily better and that over-assortment of the category can have a negative impact and confuse the customer. It is instead through providing a product line that facilitates a purchasing decision which denotes success.

Customer service is another key component to the success of any retail organization. One might ask, "How do you know if you're providing great customer service?" It is really through exceeding your sales plan. Customer service can mean many different things; it can be completing a transaction in the shortest amount of time, or it can be having all the time in the day to spend with a customer. We have a clear definition of great customer service. It is "personal and friendly." With every experience, through every transaction, the question for us remains, "Is the experience that the customer is having personal and friendly?" That is the bottom line. Personal and friendly are key traits of our brand. That definition crystallized in our company when one of our store managers was moved to a new location and someone asked his goal for the store. His goal was to have the friendliest store in town. From there, we said that's going to be the signature of our customer service.

To measure our performance in that light, we use the classic shopping services – blind shops of the store, with shoppers filling out a report card. We measure the quality of our service in numerical terms, through collecting this data. This is helpful and can point us in certain directions. Customer feedback is much easier in a catalog or even an e-commerce environment, where we can look at a number of transactions happening at one time and get a feel for how service is being provided. It is a bit more difficult with physical stores so we are constantly looking for better ways to obtain good, accurate customer feedback. It's important and it's necessary.

The Changes and Basics of Retail

I believe that there should always be a tension within a company to be both responsive to change, and to stick to your fundamentals and core proven principles. I am not a champion who has everyone looking for the latest changes, because those can lead you astray from who you are as a company and a brand. Instead, I'm an advocate for a healthy tension between the desire to do new things and the desire to stick to the proven ways of the past.

One of the most significant changes in retail since I entered the industry has been the increase in emphasis on the full customer experience. You're trying to create an experience that builds a relationship with a customer, and that experience is contained within the entire theater that you develop in your store. Department stores used to be known for the phrase "that's not my department." You would ask a sales associate for some help finding something and you'd get the stock answer "Sorry, that's not my department." That doesn't happen anymore. The biggest department store of all, Wal-Mart, has the best service. I believe that to deliver that service, the relationships that our salespeople form with customers have been brought to a whole new, wonderful level.

While the landscape has shifted a bit around the importance of location, it's still a critical part of the business that requires study. Fundamentals haven't changed too much. The old saying, "location, location, location," is still almost as true as it ever was. We know that we're never going to get it right every time, and it could be very expensive when we get it wrong. Consequently, it's critical to structure leases that offer optimum flexibility, so when it's not working, we have an out.

We use a few different approaches to gauge the best location for a new retail store, as we add to and expand upon the chain. We start with the real estate industry's demographics for a given area, and we'll overlay our catalog experience with customers in that area. Because we're a multi-channel retailer, we have great customer information on our Internet and catalog customers. In addition to this wealth of data, we've found that it's important to have a personal feel for the market and to talk to customers and nearby residents, those who understand the subtlety of the place. You have to have both macro industry information, and personal insights into the market.

Retail is the most competitive industry of all and that competition exists on so many levels. Barriers to entry are low and the number of players is huge. You can't say that about the auto industry or the world of computers. For industries such as those, the barriers to entry are so high that it is only the mega players who come in and compete. Retail takes all kinds – from college kids to anyone with an idea – so with so many players, the concepts must be that much fresher to succeed. The fundamentals of retail don't change, but the flair with which retail is executed elevates with thousands of energized people contributing on a daily basis. Knowing we're up against such nimble players keeps us coming to work every day, with our eyes wide open.

One of the most exciting things happening in the industry today is this focus on the customer experience. We are honored when a customer gives us part of their day, and we need to make that experience as fulfilling as it can be. It may be that the customer is in a hurry and looking for an efficient transaction or perhaps the customer may want more of a personal experience. My perception is that the entire industry recognizes these things, and consequently, the bar is raised on a daily basis. Retail is the most competitive industry in the world, with so many small and owner-operated companies. I can't think of a field that has more dedicated, devoted individuals who have their lives invested in their stores.

I believe the customer will tell you what changes are appropriate, but you have to listen carefully and catch the subtle messages early. We listen to our customers by taking careful notice and closely analyzing what it is that they buy, what they've stopped buying and what they don't buy. We tend to discount what they say, but we pay acute attention to what they buy. That's the clearest message we can get. We tend not to listen to what the industry says is going on, or even what customers may say in a survey. The opinion that customers express with a credit card is the most reliable opinion to go by. I'm a believer in being true to our existing customer and not chasing new customers too much. Our core customers are the ones who keep us going. They do change but we track how they are changing by keeping close scrutiny of what they're buying. It is through staying responsive to those changes and receptive to those demands that we continue to both evolve, as well as remain true to our brand and core attributes.

We accommodate change in our planning by focusing our strategies on the basic qualities of our business and not the detailed tactics. Personal and friendly customer service is a quality that is stressed in the plan. I believe if you get the quality right and stick to a budget, the rest will follow. To plan our movement forward and our strategies for the future, we start with an annual financial plan – a balance sheet and a profit and loss plan. Then, we often have two or three major initiatives related to the way we're doing business. For example, a couple of years ago, we felt that we were doing business with too broad a range of SKUs (Stock Keeping Units), so we ran an initiative to reduce that. Recently, with the economy in such a fragile state, our initiative was debt reduction. We wanted to bring down our borrowing, because in a fragile environment we don't want to be extended a whole lot. Every five years we revisit our strategic plan and make adjustments with respect to our interests, the marketplace and anything else relevant that may have a direct impact upon our business.

One change I would like to see is the closing financial transaction to happen more quickly. It seems that it is that last experience – the check-out – that is the most negative part for the customer, especially when it involves waiting in line. It's horrible that that has to be the parting experience, so there has been some movement in this area. In grocery stores, you can check yourself out now, so you're not limited by the number of cashiers available. Getting the check-out to happen more efficiently is one of my greatest wishes.

Perk Perkins has led Orvis as President and CEO since November 1992. Under his guidance, the company has grown from $88 million in sales in 1992 to nearly $300 million in 2003. Mr. Perkins has built a strong *business culture of quality and brand integrity throughout the multi-channel retailer. Orvis has prospered and earned the industry's highest awards in both Catalog and Internet marketing. Its Wholesale business holds the number one market-share position in the enthusiast fly fishing market. The Orvis Retail chain has the greatest growth potential of all the channels.*

Mr. Perkins came to work for Orvis in 1977 as the Editor of the Orvis News, Catalog Copywriter and Manager of Export Sales. He has held many other positions that have allowed him to experience the company first-hand including: Manager of the Orvis San Francisco store; President of Orvis UK; Vice President of Operations; President of Early Winters, an Orvis subsidiary; Vice President, Merchandising; and President, Orvis Mail Order.

Mr. Perkins dedicates considerable energy to conservation and serves as Vice Chairman of The Nature Conservancy, the world's largest conservation organization and the USA's 10th largest non-profit organization. For the last 25 years, he has served on boards of conservation organizations as well as local civic boards.

He graduated from Williams College, Williamstown, Massachusetts in 1975 and has completed Harvard University's Executive Management Program.

A Vision for Retailing ...

and other Points of Interest

Dick Dickson

The Paradies Shops
President & CEO

Leading Qualities in Retail

Retailing is not an easy business, especially in today's market. Today's customers are driven by different factors than in the past and are very knowledgeable about their choices.

To face this market you must bring clear statements about your brand and what the customer should expect. Then you need to deliver. The market is attracted to:

Price (Costco/Wal-Mart)
Fashion (Nordstrom's)
Convenience (Quik Trip)
Uniqueness (Host of Specialty)
Versatility (Paradies)

Included with all of these different approaches, there must be service. The Paradies Shops has grown in our industry – airport retail – because of our versatility and the level of service we deliver. It is interesting to note that less value demands higher levels of service. High value demands less levels of service, but service must exist.

Finally, the service that is provided must translate into convenience. The store layout and staffing must make it easy to shop. Customers today turn their back on any retailer that makes the shopping experience a hassle.

Service – *What is it?*

Our approach to service encompasses certain standards that at first might not be things that you normally relate to service, but definitely contribute to an overall positive customer experience. We take the customer's point of view when putting our stores merchandise plans together. Our stores are well lit, have fewer fixtures in them, and are easy to get in and out of. We make sure that we have enough cash wraps or point-of-sale stations to satisfy the peak demands. In times of low demand, it's easy to service someone; you have to be prepared to deal with the peaks when you have the most customers within a particular time. All of this is very predictable in our business, and it's very predictable for almost all retailers.

Another thing we're emphasizing is that during peak periods management should be on the sales floor. This is very important. Sometimes you'll see a big box operator with twelve cash wraps open and there will be not one person who can make a management decision. In addition, we're putting our people in brightly colored shirts. That makes it easy for the customer to find us. It's frustrating to walk into a store and not be able to identify the employees. We're trying to make everything very simple and very clean. We try to keep our cash wraps uncluttered and smaller so that we get closer to the customer. We're making sure that they have a place to put a bag down. These are small things, but at the end of the day, we know customers will have an improved shopping experience.

Even our merchandise presentation directly relates to customer service. Many companies have gone in the wrong direction in regards to presentation. They do not understand what makes a good presentation. We've analyzed what makes a store attractive and we emphasize these key things. We use the acronym C.A.L.M. "C" stands for color – we think it's very important that the store is highlighted with colorful merchandise. "A" stands for access – being able to get into the store and walk around the store easily. "L" stands for lighting – it is extremely important not only that you have a lot of lights, but that the lighting amplifies the merchandise. The last thing is maintenance – there is nothing more important. I don't care how much is spent on presentation; if stores are not well maintained, then they don't give off the right kind of image. So we use this concept called C.A.L.M., and as we look at our stores, we look at the color, the access, the lighting, and the maintenance. All four must be in place in order for us to achieve a quality presentation.

In terms of our product, we know the customer in the airport has certain basic needs. We also know that, other than these basic travel needs, the customer did not come to the airport to buy anything; he came to get on a plane. But as we said, he does have some certain basic necessities – he may need a cup of coffee and a newspaper. There's an old adage that if you've got a newspaper, a cup of coffee, and a ticket, there's probably nothing else you really need. And, in fact, that's true, so all other purchases are triggered through some kind of impulse created by the merchandise. In our stores, if a potential customer walks by and sees five people waiting in line, chances are he won't buy something he didn't need. So we try to create some impulses – make it easy to shop. We're always going to sell the newspapers, and if someone has a headache, he's going to buy aspirin from us, but we create other impulses as well. We make the customer feel comfortable that he's going to take care of his transaction rather quickly. Time is important.

The Right Approach

We really strive to focus on our execution and our performance, as opposed to what we generate on the bottom line. We are a hands-on, front-door company. Management walks into the stores just like a customer does. We shake hands with the salespeople and we evaluate what the customers are looking at. We don't go into the back office or look at the warehouse first or analyze the P&L statement. If we're doing a good job in the "front-door" areas, there is no need to work on the rest until that is accomplished and until we have met our company's standard. Our product mix is detailed by the information we have gathered from the 59 airports (330 stores) that we operate. Since the airport retail industry is so specialized, this information is also unique. When our customers come to the airport, they take on a different profile in a different environment. A cup of coffee and a newspaper might be the only two things they need, but our business cannot survive with just that revenue stream. We must create impulses with "item merchandising" that is well presented and signed. This approach results in needed additional sales that result in higher volume/profitability. The standard by which we measure that performance is called "dollars per enplanement." Every operator has to have a standard by which he can measure his performance objectively.

Remember that although we are somewhat guaranteed of traffic, we're also guaranteed that the traffic won't expand that much. If you open a store and have the best product, people from all over town will eventually come to your store. That's not the case in an airport. It doesn't matter how well you do – you're still going to have the same market potential of airline traffic. No one goes to the airport to shop. The challenge is not how to expand the market, but rather how much you sell to each passenger. In the last couple of years, we haven't had growth in traffic, but actually a loss in traffic. Through better merchandising, we are selling more products to fewer passengers and in fact we're doing more business. Selling more to fewer passengers – that's our challenge.

The Brand

The most challenging aspect of any retail chain is making sure that everyone is in step, that they are committed, and that they understand your brand and company standards. You have to make sure that this message is repeated over and over – exactly who we are and what we stand for. We emphasize that constantly. Then, after we've done that, we go out and see if people know what we're talking about. We're very decentralized here. No two stores are alike, so it's very important that the message gets down to where it counts the most. People don't always interpret things the same way. When business is good, there are two things going well: the merchandise is good and the people part is good. When it's not going well, it's either a merchandise problem or it's a people problem. Every issue in our company falls under one of those two categories. What you're constantly striving to do is get the merchandise and the people right. Good merchandising is having the right merchandise, at the right time, in the right place, in the right quantity, and at the right price (Sears & Roebuck Management Training 1967). You have to get your people committed to the goals and objectives of the company and your brand.

A successful product is one that you pay for – you sell it for a higher price than you paid for it, and there's something left over after you pay expenses. There doesn't have to be a great demand for the item – that's the beauty of this business. In retailing, you're very much in control of many things. You can affect customers' impulses and capture their interest. The reason people choose retailing (which hasn't had the greatest career path compared to many other industries) is that it gives you instant results. You get instant feedback on what you've done. It provides for a lot of excitement, enthusiasm, and recognition when you actually put something together that is successful and profitable. There are few businesses, I think, that give you that kind of feedback as quickly. You can see it happen right before your eyes. And you recognize as you gain experience in this business, if you've been trained by good merchants, that you can influence very dramatically what happens. People shrug their shoulders and say, "Hey, business is bad." Then you walk into the store and no one approaches you about the product, and you wonder how bad business really is. We believe that our destiny, to some degree anyhow, is in our hands and we are in control.

Pricing

In our stores, we're looking for the highest margin possible that does not affect the customer's opinion of our prices. Generally speaking, the higher margin you have, the better off you are as long as you are generating enough gross sales. However, we don't want to sell a pack of cigarettes for $8.00. It amazes me – you go to a five-star hotel and you pay $400 a night for a room. I don't have any problem with that, but then you go downstairs and pay $8.00 for cigarettes. I am amazed by that philosophy. They're thinking about the profitability when, in fact, it is infinitesimal compared to the overall plan. At $400 a night, they ought to give you cigarettes. It's all about perception. Can someone who pays $400 for a room afford to pay $8.00 for cigarettes? Absolutely. That has nothing to do with it. It's your perception of what they're trying to do; you're offended by it. Then, all of a sudden, you wonder "What else am I getting ripped off on?" The lesson here is that you must look at the merchandise before you figure out what the margin should be. In other words, you have to look at the merchandise and see what it will sell for.

You may purchase an item for $2.00, but you may only be able to sell it for $3.00. You cannot price an item based on a needed margin. For example, you pay $2.00 for an item and apply a 60 percent margin ($5.00). The merchandise has a perceived value that will determine what it should sell for. If you say, "I only paid $2.00 on this," and automatically sell it for $6.00 without looking at what it is, that's crazy. To go back to the cigarette example, say you're looking for a 50 percent margin; cigarettes sell for over $3.00 a pack with the taxes and everything, but if you say, "Well, that must mean I have to sell them for $7.00", that's outrageous. It's all about perceived value. Also, some merchandise is price sensitive and some merchandise is not. You know what some things cost or what they should sell for; but if, for example, I showed you the watch I have on and asked you how much it should sell for, you wouldn't have any idea. We have to be very careful. Pricing the merchandise correctly is very important.

Location, Location, Location

Location is obviously very important. We get locations in our business that aren't great, but that's where we are. We can't do anything about it, so the end result is that we're trying just as hard in a bad location as we are in a good location. But, certainly, it's important. If you have 1,000 people walking by a day and at another location you have 3,000, you ought to be doing two or three times more at the second location, assuming you're selling the same type of merchandise. We have some input on the locations we have, but after that, we set that aside and have to go to work. We focus on what customers are walking by our stores today and what we're doing about capturing them.

We look for the best terms possible in a lease. How do you get out of a location that's not working? We don't do that. All of our leases have terms and we live out the term. We are not a company that tries to get out of business. If we've made a mistake, we live with it. Certainly we try to renegotiate it and in some cases we're successful; and in some cases we're not. We have a reputation, though, and our industry is very small. Our company has been around a long time and has enjoyed uninterrupted growth and profitability. If the landlord is willing to renegotiate and he knows we're doing a good job and there are circumstances beyond our control, he will typically work with us because he has respect for us.

New Business Opportunities

The question when expanding any business is: Can you afford to do it? Is it a business plan that has a decent return to it? What does it bring to the table? It's a simple analysis. You do an estimate of what the sales and expenses are, and if it makes some sense, you consider it further. What kind of resources do you have reserved for future plans? We're very conservative. We do not make internal distributions; the profitability of the company goes back into the business. So our growth has been substantial without incurring heavy debt.

Management and Employee Relations

Our management style is very hands on. We are easy to get to and easy to talk to. We have developed a great deal of trust in our company. At all levels of management, you have to be honest with each other; otherwise you have no team or teamwork at all. Trust is the basis for every relationship in every organization. People have to know that if they've done something wrong, I'm not going to criticize them. They know that my goals and objectives are the same. They don't feel threatened by me.

People

I don't know how you find the right store managers and employees. Every employee is a risk. The key is their attitude and then their performance. Some make it and some don't. You must be sure they are committed and understand the standards the company has developed that represent the brand. If you've made it here three or four months, you'll probably be here for ten years. Because after three or four months, we know where you're coming from, we know what kind of person you are, and we know whether you understand the standard. And if you don't have those qualities, you're either with the wrong company or in the wrong business. And that never seems to change. I love to see people who have previous experience and have been with companies that spend a lot of time on training, but the bottom line is that I've had surprises on both sides.

We retain the right employees because we have a good culture. People enjoy what they do, they're enthusiastic, and they enjoy being part of a company that has a lot of respect in the industry and is considered to be the leader. They get compensated well and they get recognized; they truly feel they are part of the success.

Recognition
We have many recognition programs. For example, over the course of the year, we ask the management out in the field to present some ideas that they've come across that have impacted their business and some things we could share at the annual seminar. We have a little committee here called the Lexus Committee. This committee reviews all these ideas and sends a Lexus key to the people who've had good ideas. At the end of the year we take the four people in the company who received the most Lexus keys and, at this management seminar where there are 400 to 500 people in the audience, they draw for a real Lexus key. And whoever wins gets the use of a brand new Lexus.

We have all kinds of recognition in all kinds of categories. We have recognition programs from salespeople all the way up. We are very in tune to our salespeople, but our management is the glue that keeps this all together. These are people who have dedicated their careers to our company; when everything else fails, they'll always be there for us. I don't necessarily believe in treating everyone equal because not everyone is equal. We have great salespeople, and we recognize them too, but we try to put the emphasis on the management team.

Defining Success
Success for us is maintaining our image in the business and receiving a decent financial return. You have to be profitable – otherwise you can't continue – but I would say the real success starts with our performance in the eyes of the customer. In our case there are two customers: the person who buys things in the store and our airport management, our landlord.

Growth

We have a very strong philosophy: It does not matter how much business we do – if we do $250 million or $450 million – what matters is our profitability and the customers' perception of us. We're a private company; we're not driven by the stock market. The growth is a result of our performance. If you're a $250 million company and you're profitable, your people are taken care of, and you've got a good image, why do you have to be a $450 million company? There's no reason to be. If it comes, it's fine, if it's a result of your performance. I would say that's a major difference between private companies and public companies.

In our industry we have an expression called "PR." Most people know that as "public relations," but that's not what it means here. What it means here is "performance and relationship." If you perform and you have a good relationship, you are unbeatable. If you don't perform and have a good relationship, you are in trouble. If you do perform and have a bad relationship, you're in bigger trouble. If you don't perform and you don't have a relationship, you're dead.

I think the most successful companies out there today are being managed by people who are retailers as opposed to finance people. I think if the leadership loses touch with what's happening on the sales floor, how the system works, and what the customer needs, then they lose everything. I think many of these big companies have been driven by the financial side, and when it got down to the customer, the customer said, "Sorry, I'm not interested. You don't have anything."

To be successful, you have to stay close to the customer and make a very clear statement of what you're doing. And, obviously, all the rules of merchandising apply as well – the right merchandise, at the right price, at the right time, in the right quantity.

I love the business of retailing. I am as enthused today about it as I was 40 years ago. I am a lucky guy.

Dick graduated from Miami University at Oxford, Ohio with a B.S. in Marketing. Before joining the company in 1978, he had twenty years of retail management experience with Sears, Roebuck & Company and J.C. Penney. Dick began his employment with The Paradies Shops as Operations Manager. In 1980, he was named Vice President of Operations, responsible for overseeing the day-to-day operations of the company nationwide, and in 1982 was promoted to Senior Vice President. In May of 1994, he was promoted to President and CEO of The Paradies Shops. In addition, Dick is a stockholder of the company.

The Unique Qualities of Direct Selling

Sheila O'Connell Cooper

The Pampered Chef; Mary Kay Corp.
Former President & CEO; Former EVP & Board member

155

Direct Selling Builds Relationships

Direct selling is a business model that allows for direct interaction and face-to-face communication with the consumer of the product. In-home demonstrations, where guests see products in action and learn quick and easy tips for using the products, are an example. In the direct sales marketplace, you strive to meet the needs of your customers at their convenience – in their homes, offices and elsewhere. It's a wonderful way to bring people together, to entertain them, educate them about your products – and to sell your products.

The challenge for any direct seller is how to make the initial contact with the potential customer. But that's also the power of direct selling, because once that contact is made, it's much more significant; it's a relationship built from the beginning. Today, most people don't have the time to go a mall, to walk through the shops and figure out what they might want. With direct selling, it's likely that a sales consultant is in your customer's neighborhood, and is possibly someone they already know, who can direct them to the products they need and show them how to use those products.

The relationship you build with the consumer and your sales consultant is important. It's very much a relationship of integrity and trust. You have to be sure you are delivering what you say you are going to deliver. In all cases possible, exceed expectations. You need to be sure you're conducting business with the highest level of integrity and treating people as you would want to be treated. If you do that, it will be a successful relationship. And then you have a successful business.

The Secret of Successful Products

The products offered in direct sales must be of high quality and must have a real use in people's daily lives. Many people like to find something new and different, but those products might not be particularly useful. If you're in direct sales, you want to sell things that people will use and that won't get tucked away, unused and forgotten. You want to sell products that they'll turn to – products that meet a need, save time, and deliver an amazing result.

There are several ways to go about developing your products. Listen to your consumers who buy and use them on a daily basis, as well as your consultants who are out there demonstrating the products. One excellent strategy is to form a product advisory committee made up of members of your sales force. Of course, you will also want to search the marketplace for new and innovative ideas, and consider those which co-workers bring ideas to your attention.

By the time you bring a product to market, it should have undergone extensive tests in your test environment – laboratory, test kitchen, demonstration center – and been previewed with your consultants who can tell you how they'd like to see the product improved. There may already be a group of people who are enthusiastic endorsers of the products – consultants who have repeat customers at their in-house shows because they know they can look to the company for unique, high-quality products they'll use. Developing that level of comfort in your consultants with the products they are selling is a key success factor.

While the majority of your sales channels may be through in-home product demonstrations, don't limit your direct sales efforts just to this channel. Other channels available are catalog shows, where people can order your products from the catalog, and fundraiser shows to benefit charitable organizations. Depending on your product, consider other types of exposure – bridal shows, cooking classes, crafts parties, cosmetic "make-over" parties. The opportunities to sell your products are limited only by your imagination and the type of product you offer.

One of the wonderful things about a direct-selling model is that, inherent to the model, it has a relationship of trust with the customer, something that traditional retailers are constantly trying to establish. The sales consultants already have relationships with the customers; often they are their neighbors, their friends, their relatives, or friends of friends. When somebody purchases a product through direct sales, they often do so from a person they know, so if they have a question about it, they can ask. It's unlike a traditional retailer, when the person who helped you the first time is nowhere to be found after that, much less available to come to your home and ensure your satisfaction with the product.

Managing the Team, Near and Far

When you establish a friendly working environment, your direct sales consultants have fun and show that this form of retail is such a great way to build relationships. Then people may feel comfortable approaching your consultants to learn about joining your company. They'll see it as a way of doing something they love, interacting with people and teaching them about your product – as well as making money.

Amazingly, you may not even have to advertise for people to join your company. Your consultants can create such a desire that people approach them because they appreciate the opportunity that working for a direct selling company represents. It's a flexible work schedule; they decide when and if they want to work. There is no specific required level of education, expertise, or financial resources because you offer all the training. It's a great way to earn extra income and socialize with people.

Typically, someone who joins a company in direct sales has been to at least one gathering or demonstration where the company's products have been sold. They have seen a consultant host a show, talk about the products, and use them before an audience.

In many direct selling organizations, the investment in entering into the business is minimal. For a small sum, usually under $100, they get a kit filled with products they can use in demonstrations, as well as a number of training materials (videos, audiotapes, and written materials) that teach them about the product, how to hold a party or demonstration, and how to use the products to their best advantage. And the person they approached about joining the company is likely to be available to help, too.

Motivating People to Obtain their Goals

In many ways the goals of sales consultants are self-determined, depending on the amount of time and effort they want to put into the business. As they put more time and effort into the business, companies typically offer levels of leadership in the sales field that they can achieve. They start at the sales consultant level and can advance all the way up to a national-level senior executive. Along the way they earn commissions, and many direct sales companies offer additional incentives – trips, cruises, jewelry, and production bonuses, for example.

In this business, it is rare that you might accomplish something wonderful on your own; instead, you do it with a team of people. If you make sure you meet the needs of your sales consultants, who are actually independent contractors, they will help ensure your company's success. Every department in your company should understand that its primary goal and role is to support the efforts of your sales people out in the field.

Communication can be a significant motivator. You might consider publishing a newsletter to keep your sales force informed about things happening in your business and industry, recognize individual achievements, and provide updates on products.

Conferences are another motivating opportunity; if your budget allows, holding conferences at different times of the year, for different purposes, and targeting different audiences can help drive your success. Several companies structure their conferences to different levels of their sales organizations, for example:

A national conference each year that all people in the sales force are eligible to attend and that might offer sales recognition, training on new products, and workshops

Leadership conferences for people in your sales force who have reached a certain level of commitment – management, for instance, or full-time sales, rather than part-time, with a serious focus on growing their businesses

Throughout the year, a number of programs where people from your corporate offices travel throughout the country and work with your sales consultants to offer training and support for those who can't travel to your other conferences

The Challenges of Effective Management

The hardest challenge in managing a direct sales organization is communication. You need constant, consistent, and effective communication. You need to build the reality that people know they can count on you to do what you say you're going to do, that you lead with integrity, and that you live up to their trust.

People who are willing to take the initiative and run with a project are always appreciated. To foster that type of behavior, you have to allow people to manage and not become too intrusive into their day-to-day work. You can be a ready resource for everyone you work with, and be engaged in all that they do, but I've found it's best to let people invite your advice, unless you notice something going astray. Part of the criteria for joining your team should be a strong need to take responsibility.

Finding good people is difficult. You have to spend a lot of time talking and listening to them to determine whether they share a vision and a goal similar to the rest of the team. What I call the human side, or the personal skills, are every bit as important as technical skills. That's true especially in a business like direct selling, which depends on building good relationships. I think people stay with a team when they feel recognized and valued, and where they are given opportunities to grow and become strong leaders in their own right. When you create an atmosphere like that and you trust people, people will exceed your expectations. When you establish an atmosphere where people can be creative and not worry about internal office politics, you create a strong team that can meet any challenge.

Many managers take great joy in watching people on the team reach for the next level of their development. It's a challenge to see how you can grow the business and better support your consultants and customers. As a manager, you should work hard to offer opportunities for the people on your sales force, and to operate with high ethics and integrity. Being affiliated with a company that does the right thing gives people a sense of pride. Beyond that, challenge people to step out of their comfort zones. Direct sales, regardless of your product, is an ever-changing marketplace, and the last thing you can do is rest on your laurels. Never be satisfied with the status quo.

Your company's reputation is a strong indicator of its success; strive for a reputation for ethics and integrity and high-quality products. Another indicator of success: return customers. If customers come back to you again and again to purchase products because they are your brand, that's an excellent sign. One of the more profound indicators of your company's success is the success of your salespeople in meeting their own goals. You can also see success through the growth of employees inside the company – those who start at entry-level positions and move up to positions of increasing responsibility.

The Changing Direct Sales Market

Demands on consumers' time have changed dramatically. People have less time to look at opportunities and consider new products. They are appreciative of someone who can save them time, help them find products of high quality, and provide a real service.

The way people are willing to purchase items has also changed. There was a time when everyone wanted to walk into a store and touch something before they bought it. Now, people are much more comfortable buying items over the Internet. The way people communicate has changed dramatically. All of those changes mean that the way we communicate and share information and the time we take to share that information also has had to change. Everyone, regardless of the business they're in, has had to become much more respectful of the fact that people want to get all the same information, but they want it short, concise, and delivered in a convenient manner.

Every company has to position itself to thrive on change if it wants to continue to grow. You don't have to change things every day, but you have to be open to the fact that things are changing, and you have to be ready to adapt to those changes. A company that is slow to change will not be as successful as it could be.

It helps to take advantage of many different sources of information to keep up with the changes in your industry. Go to trade shows, belong to trade associations, and encourage feedback from consultants and customers. Try spending time on the weekends walking through stores, seeing how salespeople communicate with their customers, looking at the quality of their products, the price points of the products and what seem to be the current trends. Those are keys, as are observing people and listening to your neighbors and friends to see what's sparking their interest and where they're willing to spend their time.

Believing in Your Product, Acting With Integrity

To succeed in the direct sales business, you need to believe in your product and to believe you are adding value through what you're bringing to the marketplace. Further, I personally believe, quite strongly, in the power of direct selling. I believe in what it brings to the consumer, that it delivers a high-quality product and a level of service people cannot get in the more traditional retail setting. I'm passionate about it because I love watching sales consultants grow as a result of their involvement in the business. I'm constantly motivated and inspired by watching people bring added value to other peoples' lives. Direct selling is a unique vehicle in making that happen.

Sheila O'Connell Cooper is the former President and CEO of The Pampered Chef. O'Connell Cooper first joined The Pampered Chef family in January 2001 as president and chief operating officer. In January 2003, she was named president and chief executive officer, reporting directly to Berkshire Hathaway's Warren Buffett and was responsible for the corporate strategic and operational decisions of the multi-million dollar international company.

During her tenure with the company, O'Connell Cooper was influential in the growth and success of the organization. She directed the acquisition of The Pampered Chef by Berkshire Hathaway, successfully launched a new line of tabletop products called Simple Additions™ and spearheaded the opening of a new 780,000-square-foot international headquarters. O'Connell Cooper also helped to promote The Pampered Chef's mealtime message and vision for Kitchen Consultants, hosts and customers worldwide.

O'Connell Cooper's direct selling experience began in 1988 when she joined the Mary Kay Corp., Dallas, and became executive vice president and a member of its board of directors. During her 11 years at Mary Kay, sales more than tripled. In 1999, she became president and chief operating officer of BeautiControl, Inc., a global direct-selling company headquartered in Dallas. She established and implemented the strategic direction for the company's global operations and completed the successful acquisition of BeautiControl by Tupperware.

Sheila O'Connell Cooper currently serves on the Board of Directors of the Direct Selling Association (DSA) and the Direct Selling Education Foundation (DSEF). She holds a law degree from Southern Methodist University Law School in Dallas and a bachelor of science degree from the University of Maryland, College Park.

EXECUTIVE REPORTS

Targeted Reports Written by Hundreds of C-Level Executives

Executive Reports: How to Get an Edge as an Entrepreneur

This insider look at the entrepreneurial profession is written by CEOs of over 50 of the fastest growing private companies. Each CEO shares their knowledge on how to get an edge as an entrepreneur, from time management to breaking into new industries to building your team. Also covered are over 250 specific, proven innovative entrepreneurial strategies and methodologies practiced by leading entrepreneurs and CEOs of the world that have helped them gain an edge. This report is designed to give you insight into the leading entrepreneurs of the world, and assist you in developing additional "special skills" that can help you be even more successful as an entrepreneur. $295– 120 Pages, 8.5 x 11

Executive Reports: Board Member Liabilities & Responsibilities

This insider look at board membership is the ideal tool for current board members to understand the new liabilities and responsibilities of being part of a board of directors. Current board members from Wal-Mart, 3M, Brystol Myers Squibb, Georgia Pacific, Phillip Morris, Mattel, Lowe's, Wachovia and Heidrick & Struggles share their knowledge on board membership, responsibilities and the new requirements given the increasing focus on corporate governance. Also highlighted are new ethics and privacy regulations that every board member needs to be aware of, or face excess liabilities and exposure. $279 – 70 Pages, 8.5x11

BEST SELLING BOOKS

Visit Your Local Bookseller Today or www.Aspatore.com For More Information

REFERENCE

Small Business Bible – Phone Numbers, Business Resources, Financial, Tax & Legal Info
The Small Business Checkup – A Planning & Brainstorming Workbook for Your Business
Business Travel Bible – Must Have Phone Numbers, Business Resources & Maps
The Golf Course Locator for Business Professionals – Golf Courses Closest to Largest Companies, Law Firms, Cities & Airports
Business Grammar, Style & Usage – Rules for Articulate and Polished Business Writing and Speaking
ExecRecs – Executive Recommendations For The Best Business Products & Services
Living Longer Working Stronger – Simple Steps for Business Professionals to Capitalize on Better Health
The C-Level Test – Business IQ & Personality Test for Professionals of All Levels
The Business Translator-Business Words, Phrases & Customs in Over 65 Languages

MANAGEMENT

Corporate Ethics – The Business Code of Conduct for Ethical Employees
The Governance Game – Restoring Boardroom Excellence & Credibility in America
Inside the Minds: Leading CEOs – CEOs Reveal the Secrets to Leadership & Profiting in Any Economy
Inside the Minds: The Entrepreneurial Problem Solver – Entrepreneurial Strategies for Identifying Opportunities in the Marketplace
Inside the Minds: Leading Consultants – Industry Leaders Share Their Knowledge on the Art of Consulting
Being There Without Going There: Managing Teams Across Time Zones, Locations and Corporate Boundaries

TECHNOLOGY

Inside the Minds: Leading CTOs – The Secrets to the Art, Science & Future of Technology
Software Product Management – Managing Software Development from Idea to Development to Marketing to Sales
Inside the Minds: The Telecommunications Industry – Leading CEOs Share Their Knowledge on The Future of the Telecommunications Industry
Web 2.0 AC (After Crash) – The Resurgence of the Internet and Technology Economy
Inside the Minds: The Semiconductor Industry – Leading CEOs Share Their Knowledge on the Future of Semiconductors

VENTURE CAPITAL/ENTREPRENEURIAL

Term Sheets & Valuations – A Detailed Look at the Intricacies of Term Sheets & Valuations
Deal Terms – The Finer Points of Deal Structures, Valuations, Term Sheets, Stock Options and Getting Deals Done
Inside the Minds: The Ways of the VC – Identifying Opportunities, Assessing Business Models and What it Takes to Land an Investment From a VC

To Order or For Customized Suggestions From an Aspatore Business Editor,
Please Call 1-866-Aspatore (277-2867) Or
Visit www.Aspatore.com

Inside the Minds: Leading Deal Makers – Leveraging Your Position and the Art of Deal Making

Inside the Minds: Entrepreneurial Momentum – Gaining Traction for Businesses of All Sizes to Take the Step to the Next Level

Inside the Minds: The Entrepreneurial Problem Solver – Entrepreneurial Strategies for Identifying Opportunities in the Marketplace

Inside the Minds: JumpStart – Launching Your Business Venture, Profitably and Successfully

LEGAL

Inside the Minds: Privacy Matters – Leading Privacy Visionaries Share Their Knowledge on How Privacy on the Internet Will Affect Everyone

Inside the Minds: Leading Lawyers – Leading Managing Partners Reveal the Secrets to Professional and Personal Success as a Lawyer

Inside the Minds: The Innovative Lawyer – Leading Lawyers Share Their Knowledge on Using Innovation to Gain an Edge

Inside the Minds: Leading Labor Lawyers – Labor Chairs Reveal the Secrets to the Art & Science of Labor Law

Inside the Minds: Leading Litigators – Litigation Chairs Revel the Secrets to the Art & Science of Litigation

Inside the Minds: Leading IP Lawyers – IP Chairs Reveal the Secrets to the Art & Science of IP Law

Inside the Minds: Leading Deal Makers – The Art of Negotiations & Deal Making

Inside the Minds: The Corporate Lawyer – Corporate Chairs on the Successful Practice of Business Law

FINANCIAL

Inside the Minds: Leading Accountants – The Golden Rules of Accounting & the Future of the Accounting Industry and Profession

Inside the Minds: Leading Investment Bankers – Leading I-Bankers Reveal the Secrets to the Art & Science of Investment Banking

Inside the Minds: The Financial Services Industry – The Future of the Financial Services Industry & Professions

Building a $1,000,000 Nest Egg – 10 Strategies to Gaining Wealth at Any Age

Inside the Minds: The Return of Bullish Investing

Inside the Minds: The Invincibility Shield for Investors

MARKETING/ADVERTISING/PR

Inside the Minds: Leading Marketers–Leading Chief Marketing Officers Reveal the Secrets to Building a Billion Dollar Brand

Inside the Minds: Leading Advertisers – Advertising CEOs Reveal the Tricks of the Advertising Profession

Inside the Minds: The Art of PR – Leading PR CEOs Reveal the Secrets to the Public Relations Profession

Inside the Minds: PR Visionaries – PR CEOS Reveal the Golden Rules to Becoming a Senior Partner With Your Clients

Inside the Minds: The Art of Building a Brand – Leading Advertising & PR CEOs Reveal the Secrets Behind Successful Branding Strategies

The Best of Guerrilla Marketing – Marketing on a Shoestring Budget

To Order or For Customized Suggestions From an Aspatore Business Editor, Please Call 1-866-Aspatore (277-2867) Or Visit www.Aspatore.com

ASPATORE BOOKS

BULK/CUSTOMIZED BOOK ORDERS

Aspatore Books offers discount pricing and customization of cover art and text on bulk orders. Customization choices might include but are not limited to: Adding your logo to the spine and cover; Personalizing the book title to include your company's name; Removing specific unwanted content; Adding a letter from your CEO or others; Including an application form or other collateral materials. Companies use Aspatore books for a variety of purposes, including: Customer Acquisition, Customer Retention, Incentives and Premiums, Employee and Management Education. Contact Rachel Pollock at 617.742.8988 or rp@aspatore.com for more information.

LICENSE CONTENT FROM THIS BOOK

Aspatore content is often licensed for publications, web sites, newsletters and more. Electronic licenses are also available to make an entire book (or series of books) available for employees and/or customers via your web site. Please contact Jason Edwards at jason@aspatore.com for more information.

ADVERTISE IN C-LEVEL BUSINESS REVIEW

Every quarter, C-Level Business Review reaches thousands of the leading decision makers in the United States. Subscribers to the magazine include C-Level executives (CEO, CFO, CTO, CMO, Partner) from over half the Global 500 and top 200 largest law firms. Please email jonp@aspatore.com for advertising rates and more information.

CORPORATE PUBLISHING GROUP
(AN ASPATORE OWNED COMPANY)

Corporate Publishing Group (CPG) provides companies with on-demand writing and editing resources from the world's best writing teams. Our clients come to CPG for the writing and editing of books, reports, speeches, company. For more information please e-mail rpollock@corporateapublishinggroup.com.

For a Complete Electronic Catalogue of Aspatore Books, Products & Services, Please Email jennifer@aspatore.com

To Order or For Customized Suggestions From an Aspatore Business Editor, Please Call 1-866-Aspatore (277-2867) Or Visit www.Aspatore.com

INSIDE THE MINDS:
The Art of Retail

Acknowledgements and Dedications

Whitney Anderson – I'd like to thank my fabulous wife Cathy and son Maxwell for their unwavering support, insight and encouragement through all our business' ups and downs, and thank my incredibly dedicated and creative partners Dave Clark, Dan Krebs, and Ed Fortune without whom we would have neither a business nor this chapter.

Sheila O'Connell Cooper – To my hero, my husband, Ken Cooper, who encourages and inspires me every day, to my parents for teaching me to never give up and to Mary Kay Ash, founder of Mary Kay Inc., who taught me so very much but most of all the power of believing.

Steve Puett – I would like to dedicate this chapter to my wife, Suzanne, and our children, Taylor and Casey, whose unconditional love and support (and occasional subtle reminder of what is truly most important in life...faith, family, and friends) provide an endless supply of inspiration and foundational support.

ASPATORE
BOOKS

C-LEVEL BUSINESS INTELLIGENCE · C-LEVEL BUSINESS INTELLIGENCE ·